"When you've experienced lc
God invites us to hope, to da
and our broken dreams. If you're holding this book in your hands,
you've known that loss (or you love someone who has) and yet, the
hope of new life is also upon you. You've come to the right place. Teske
is someone who has personally walked this journey. She cares deeply
about you and wants to help you sort through all that you're feeling
during this time. She'll walk beside you as a trusted friend and she'll
remind you every step of the way that God is with you and He will
not forsake you. May the Lord Himself meet you in the pages of this
precious book."

—**Susie Larson**, national radio host,
author of *Your Beautiful Purpose*

"I wish this book had been available when I was pregnant after loss!
Teske hits on all of the major emotions women tend to experience
in a subsequent pregnancy—fear, uncertainty, worry, hope, and joy
among them. The stories she shares from her own life and from others
who have walked this path reassure her readers that such emotions are
normal, but she doesn't leave us there. Instead, she points us to Jesus,
not our circumstances, as the true source of hope and joy and peace—
something that encourages me as I now parent my two living miracles.
I look forward very much to sharing this book with the women I
encounter in my Naomi's Circle ministry and strongly recommend it
to others seeking encouragement in this journey."

—**Kristi Bothur**, MEd, founder of Naomi's Circle ministry and
contributing editor of *Rainbows and Redemption: Encouragement for
the Journey of Pregnancy After Loss*

"*Expecting with Hope* is a gift! Not many people understand the complex emotions of pregnancy after loss, but Teske Drake has been there

and it shows. She guides readers through God's Word with tenderness and transparency. Both her personal stories and the stories she shares of other real-life moms will encourage and inspire. This book will be my go-to resource when ministering to expectant moms after loss."

—**Becky Avella,** author of *And Then You Were Gone: Restoring a Broken Heart After Pregnancy Loss*

"Teske Drake knows the anguish of losing a child. She also knows where to take her cracked heart in order to make it whole again. Her honest and helpful book will allow you to regain your joy—finding purpose in your pain and grace among the grit."

—**Karen Ehman**, Proverbs 31 Ministries; author of seven books including *LET. IT. GO.: How to Stop Running the Show & Start Walking in Faith*; and mom of three on earth and one in heaven

EXPECTING
with
HOPE

EXPECTING
with
HOPE

*Claiming Joy When
Expecting a Baby
After Loss*

Teske Drake

Kregel
Publications

Expecting with Hope: Claiming Joy When Expecting a Baby After Loss
© 2014 by Teske Drake

Published by Kregel Publications, a division of Kregel, Inc., 2450 Oak Industrial Dr. NE, Grand Rapids, MI 49505.

Published in association with the literary agency of Credo Communications, LLC, Grand Rapids, Michigan, www.credocommunications.net.

The stories shared in this book were collected through interviews conducted by the author. The women whose stories are represented have provided written consent for their stories, names, and children's names to be published in this book.

The author and publisher are not engaged in rendering medical or psychological services, and this book is not intended as a guide to diagnose or treat medical or psychological problems. If medical, psychological, or other expert assistance is required by the reader, please seek the services of your own physician or certified counselor.

ISBN   978-0-8254-4337-4

Printed in the United States of America
14 15 16 17 18 / 5 4 3 2 1

For Gabe and Aiyana . . . my two living miracles

❧ ❦

Contents

Foreword

There is great joy and reason for celebration when a baby is expected to enter this world. However, I have experienced firsthand that pregnancy doesn't always go as planned. We experienced a miscarriage early on in our childbearing years, as well as the loss of our most recent child, Jubilee, at eighteen weeks along. The pain of pregnancy loss is one that stays in a mother's heart and is an experience that no future child could ever erase. God has made each child one-of-a-kind and graces us, as mothers, with the ability to love each one uniquely.

Throughout the pages of this book Teske Drake shares, with her voice of empathy and experience, words of encouragement in the mix of emotions that you may feel as you experience pregnancy another time around. Like me—and like you—Teske knows the difficulty of loss and the joy of motherhood, and she faithfully reminds us that God has given His Word and the promises contained in it to help us on our motherhood journey and to point us to the source of all hope, joy, and peace—Jesus!

—Michelle Duggar
Mom of TLC's *19 Kids & Counting*

Preface

"When do you think you'll start to try again?" I despised this question. For a time, I didn't know if we'd ever "try again." To do so meant that we'd have to be vulnerable, take risks, and maybe even experience loss again. Fear paralyzed me from the thought of it, and for a season I was perfectly content with having one child to raise. My firstborn son, Gabe, was just four years old when his baby sister, Chloe, died and went to be with Jesus.

Chloe was diagnosed in utero with a chromosomal abnormality (interstitial deletion of chromosome 2) and the accompanying brain condition, holoprosencaphaly. The prognosis was 100 percent fatal. We carried her as long as possible, until my body went into premature labor at thirty-two weeks along—labor that couldn't be stopped. Chloe was born on May 11, 2006, and lived for forty-five minutes before she breathed her last and was ushered into the presence of Jesus: life-giver, life-sustainer, my one true source of all hope. The experience shook me to the core, but I did the only thing I knew to do and turned to the God of all hope: my God who had been there all along, even though I had turned my back on Him years ago. He was faithful to meet me in the depths of my grief, in the hard places of perseverance, and provided me with a strength that could only come from Him. Through Chloe's birth and death, ministry was born.

More than a year later, my husband and I began to pray about whether another child was part of our future as a family. For months we prayed for wisdom and discernment, trusting the Lord's leading in our lives. Within just a few weeks of sensing that it was time to try again—something I wasn't quite sure we'd ever be ready for—we learned that we were expecting. Nine months later, Aiyana entered this world as a healthy baby girl who is five (going on fifteen) as I write these words.

The year that followed brought with it a desire for more children. What ensued, however, was more grief. We became pregnant easily—something I certainly do not take for granted, having ministered to many who struggle with fertility challenges. Yet sustaining pregnancy happened to be my particular challenge. I experienced two miscarriages; one at six weeks and another at fourteen weeks—Jesse and Riyah Mae, two more precious children in heaven whom I love and long for. Shortly after these losses, we came to the conclusion that our childbearing days were through. While we haven't made any permanent decisions or taken any physical actions to prevent pregnancy from happening in the future, we feel a great sense of peace that our family is complete.

I share my story with you so that you know I am a mother who can empathize with the mixed emotions you are experiencing as you embark upon this pregnancy journey. While no two pregnancies are ever alike, the painful experience of miscarriage or infant loss brings many lingering emotions and fears into the experience of subsequent pregnancy. As another mother has said so clearly, "The joy and innocence of pregnancy is lost." It is my great hope that we can walk this road together, deal with the grief that's always there, and claim joy along the way. Thanks for trusting me to come alongside you on this journey.

Introduction

Perfect Peace

peace in the promise ⸺

You will keep in perfect peace those whose minds are steadfast, because they trust in you.

ISAIAH 26:3

Breathe in. Breathe out. Deep breath. Repeat.

Let me start out by saying this: I'm proud of you. Yes, you. The one who is reading this book and can't believe it herself.

I'm guessing it took a lot of courage to pick up this book. Or maybe picking up the book wasn't so bad, but opening its pages was a whole other story. And oh, to read the words . . . have mercy! Because to open up this book and to read the words printed here on these pages means one very exciting (and scary, mind-boggling, crazy) thing for you: you're pregnant. Again.

And not just any old again, but pregnant after having had the painful experience of loss—whether by miscarriage, stillbirth, or infant loss—and so now, to pick up a book about pregnancy, well there are some pretty major implications. To read a book about pregnancy means first and foremost that you are, to some degree, ready and willing to embark on this journey. Ready or not, the baby is growing as the Lord continues to knit and weave this little one's precious body together in your womb. Fellow mommy and my sweet friend Sarah, who has walked this road, wisely prayed, "Keep knitting, Lord."

As He knits away in the secret place (Ps. 139:13, 15), I want you to know that I consider it a great honor and absolute joy to be able to take you by the hand and walk this journey with you. We are going to spend quite some time together, digging deep into some real and relevant biblical promises that I pray are of great encouragement to you along the way. With the Lord's guidance, it is my great hope that you are able to claim joy amidst the grief as a mommy who is *expecting with hope*.

What This Book Is and Is Not

Let's be clear from the beginning as to what this book is *not*. It's not a one-size-fits-all approach to dealing with pregnancy after loss. I can't offer you any magic formula, super fab prenatal vitamin, or stress-eliminating strategies that will replace every unpleasant emotion with pure joy. I wish I could. I would love to see women spared from the pain of grief and the torment of anxiety that accompanies pregnancy after loss.

But in a way, I'm glad I can't, because I have the absolute joy of introducing you to the giver of every good and perfect gift (James 1:17), the God and Father of our Lord Jesus Christ. It is God who grants peace. It is God who brings healing. It is God who delivers and redeems. The purpose of this book is to guide you into a relationship with God that brings peace: first for your weary soul and second for your circumstances. God offers such peace to us—*perfect peace*—as we place our trust in Him. Peace with God comes by way of the cross of His Son Jesus Christ. Let me introduce you to Jesus, the Prince of Peace (appendix A). Jesus will be our guide throughout these pages. It is my hope and prayer that you follow Him each and every step of the way, and that your first steps will lead you to your knees in surrender. Jesus longs to be your peace and to bring you peace.

How to Use This Book

Each chapter of this book focuses on a different promise from Scripture as it relates to the experience of pregnancy after miscarriage, stillbirth, or infant loss. Bible verses, which I call *Peace in the Promise*, as well as my own story and the stories of other women, are interspersed throughout the teaching of each chapter. *Pregnancy prayers* will help guide you into a quiet time with the Lord. In addition, each chapter concludes with one week's worth of five devotions, including a *pregnancy promise*, relevant Scripture, a short anecdote, prayer, and a journaling prompt called *pen the promise* to help you apply the devotions to your own situation. I encourage you to be honest in your responses, and write them down. Recording your responses will allow you to eventually add them to your child's baby book, if you so choose.

The Promise of a Hope and a Future

"For I know the plans I have for you," declares the LORD, "plans to prosper you and not to harm you, plans to give you hope and a future."

JEREMIAH 29:11

You open the first pages to find yet another cliché: God has a plan and a purpose. If you're reading this book, you've no doubt heard such clichés a time or two before as you trudged through the pain of grief (and perhaps still are). Well-intentioned loved ones, friends, and acquaintances offered up clichés like:

It was God's plan.
I'm sure it's for the better.
Heaven needed another angel.

I imagine you recognize these clichés and, sadly, can probably expand upon this list far beyond what I could manage to think up on my own. I'm sorry that you've endured the experience of miscarriage or infant loss. It's an isolating experience. My hope for us, in the time that we will spend together traveling through these pages, is that we can sift through the messiness of grief and embrace moments of joy along this journey of pregnancy after loss.

Hear the depths of my heart when I present this truth to you: there *is* a hope and a future. God's Word tells us clearly, as we saw in our peace-in-the-promise Bible verse from Jeremiah. God knows the plans for our future, which consist of hope, not harm. I can't guarantee that this means a carefree, full-term pregnancy resulting in a healthy baby. Quite frankly, that's a promise I wouldn't dare make, though it is my deepest desire for you. But I can guarantee that God's Word is true, real, and relevant for each and every one of us, regardless of our circumstances in life.

In the gospel of John, chapter 17, Jesus was praying for His disciples. He asked God the Father to "Sanctify them by the truth" and went on to declare, "Your word is truth" (John 17:17). Jesus Himself was acknowledging to God that His Word is true. Paul's second letter to Timothy states that "All Scripture is God-breathed and is useful for teaching, rebuking, correcting and training in righteousness, so that the servant of God may be thoroughly equipped for every good work" (2 Tim. 3:16–17). I point these verses out so that we may know that God's Word is true; it's "alive and active" (Heb. 4:12) and is not mere cliché. With this truth in mind—the authority and accuracy of God's Holy Word—we will delve into a deeper understanding of who God is and of the peace He brings through His promises.

Your Creator Knows You

I've found words from Psalm 139 to be a healing balm to my hurting soul in the aftermath of loss, reminding me of God's loving involvement in each of my babies' lives:

Expecting with Hope

For you created my inmost being;
    you knit me together in my mother's womb.
I praise you because I am fearfully and wonderfully made;
    your works are wonderful,
    I know that full well.
My frame was not hidden from you
    when I was made in the secret place,
    when I was woven together in the depths of the earth.
Your eyes saw my unformed body;
    all the days ordained for me were written in your book
    before one of them came to be. (vv. 13–16)

It's possible these verses have been of comfort to you, as well, as you've grieved over the loss of your baby prior to this pregnancy. And as I say *grieved over,* by no means do I intend to imply that your grief is over. Rather the idea of grieving over my babies illuminates painful memories of many nights I spent hunched over with emptiness, longing, and pain for my three little ones who are in heaven. The hard work of grief—yes, it is work—is a continuous process.

These words from Psalm 139 that have brought comfort during times of mourning have also brought me hope and encouragement in times of expectation, especially as I think back to the time of my pregnancy with Aiyana, our precious daughter, born after Chloe who is in heaven. Just as I had been comforted in my loss by the truth that God knew each day that was ordained for Chloe before it came to be, I gleaned comfort in knowing that the life of Aiyana, my unborn child, was also in His hands. As keenly as He knew both of them, He also knew me. He knew my fears, my anxieties, my hopes, and my dreams, and He loved me more than I could fathom. I had to let these truths sink into the depths of my soul as I wrestled with God's good plan and questioned whether He truly had a future and a hope for me.

While these verses from the middle of Psalm 139 are of great comfort and encouragement, it's important that we examine the psalm from the beginning. The psalmist, King David, begins by declaring:

You have searched me, LORD,
 and you know me.
You know when I sit and when I rise;
 you perceive my thoughts from afar.
You discern my going out and my lying down;
 you are familiar with all my ways.
Before a word is on my tongue
 you, LORD, know it completely.
You hem me in behind and before,
 and you lay your hand upon me.
Such knowledge is too wonderful for me,
 too lofty for me to attain.

Where can I go from your Spirit?
 Where can I flee from your presence?
If I go up to the heavens, you are there;
 if I make my bed in the depths, you are there.
If I rise on the wings of the dawn,
 if I settle on the far side of the sea,
even there your hand will guide me,
 your right hand will hold me fast.
If I say, "Surely the darkness will hide me
 and the light become night around me,"
even the darkness will not be dark to you;
 the night will shine like the day,
 for darkness is as light to you. (vv. 1–12)

These verses paint a beautiful picture of how intimately our Creator God knows the psalmist. These words also convey His intimate knowledge of each and every one of us.

                Expecting with Hope

Consider how you might apply the truth from these verses into your daily life as a woman who is expecting with hope . . .

When two pink lines appear, He is there.
    When you don't know whether to rejoice or mourn, He is there.
When you hear that first heartbeat,
    He is there.
When you grumble over morning sickness—
    then thank Him that you have it—He is there.
When you see those first glimpses of your little one through ultrasound,
    He is there.
When your mind races with what-ifs,
    He is there.
When you struggle with guilt over embracing a tinge of joy,
    all the while missing your little one(s) in heaven,
    He is there.
When you lie in wait for movement,
    holding your breath with each and every kick,
    He is there.
On that day when your precious child enters this world,
    there too, He will be.

With each of these moments, in every thought, worry, fear, and celebration, He is there. We will dive deeper into the promise of His presence in chapter 3, but for now, take heart as you rest in the knowledge that God knows you intimately and has a future and a hope in store.

With All Your Heart

God's hope and future for you is not some far-off promise. The promise of a hope and a future is a promise to embrace right now, in the present. We began this chapter with the words, "'For I know the plans I have for you,' declares the Lord, 'plans to prosper you and not to harm you, plans to give you hope and a future'" (Jer. 29:11). That chapter of God's Word goes on to unveil the key to this promised hope and future: "Then you will call on me and come and pray to me, and I will listen to you. You will seek me and find me when you seek me with all your heart" (vv. 12–13). This is a promise to embrace now, in these very moments of seeking. God is calling you to seek Him with all your heart. All of it. And when you seek Him with all your heart, He is sure to be found, just as His Word proclaims.

If you're anything like me, seeking with all your heart can be a bit of a challenge. Not because you don't desire to seek God, His will, or His plan and purpose. Truly, I constantly long for that. But I struggle in giving it *all* to Him. At times life has been filled with turmoil, heart-aches have taken me into the deep, and worry has gotten the best of me. Sure, circumstances in life have something to do with it, but not nearly as much as the circumstances of my heart. When I'm seeking God with all my heart, trusting in Him and who He says He is, I truly experience perfect peace. My circumstances may not change, but my perspective sure does.

In contrast, if I'm trying to guard my heart with my own strength, then I'm not truly seeking God with all that I am and all that He's asked of me. As a result, I fail to let Him be my peace. We need to allow the peace of God to rule in our hearts and let Him do the work of standing guard. He withholds no good thing from those whose walk is blameless, according to Psalm 84:11. It's difficult to seek God wholeheartedly and trust Him rather than ourselves, especially when it comes to the life of our child. Thanks be to God for His patience and His mercy in our lives; He is with us when we wonder (worry) and when we wander (stray).

peace in the promise _____

And the peace of God, which transcends all understanding, will guard your hearts and your minds in Christ Jesus.

PHILIPPIANS 4:7

Expecting with Hope

Wondering . . . and Wandering

There will be times, and likely have been already, when wondering and wandering become part of your experience while pregnant after a loss. You may be wondering what in the world I mean by these two words that sound so much alike, yet contrast in meaning. Let's explore.

Wondering. According to Merriam-Webster, the primary definition for wondering is, "to be in a state of wonder" or "to feel surprise." This could describe many of us at hearing the news of our pregnancy, whether we were "trying" or not. As a mother whose living children are twelve and six years old, I remain in a state of wonder when I watch them interact; see them run off the bus, across the front yard, and into our home, racing to get to me first; or gaze on them when they are fast asleep. It's an amazing, awesome thing to be entrusted by the Creator with the care of these little ones, starting from the moment they are conceived. God chose me to be the mother to all five of my children; three in heaven and two here on earth. God chose you to be the mother of your little ones as well; those whom you've had to say good-bye to, those who may already be in your care, and this little one who now grows within. My, the wonders of an unborn baby growing and developing in a mother's womb, reliant upon her for his or her every need. Yes, this is a wonder!

A secondary definition of *wondering* offered up by Merriam-Webster is, "to feel curiosity or doubt." Bingo. This may be more like the wonder you can relate to as you journey through pregnancy after loss. Wondering thoughts tend to permeate our minds, our hearts, and our reactions to every physical symptom (or lack thereof) that we experience. During my pregnancy with Aiyana, I recall wondering whether she would also be diagnosed with a chromosomal abnormality, as her sister Chloe was. Even after the ultrasound revealed a healthy, growing baby girl, I wondered whether she would be born alive. Given my past experience with loss, wondering in this manner seemed to be the default. Such thoughts have the potential to consume us if we aren't careful.

Wandering. Merriam-Webster defines wandering as "to move about without a fixed course, aim, or goal; to go idly by." In pregnancy, we certainly have a fixed course in mind: forty weeks of smooth sailing, periodic appointments, and milestone moments resulting in a full-term, healthy baby. Those of us who've endured loss know well that there is no fixed course in pregnancy. Our naïveté died just as quickly as our precious babies left our wombs. So to say that we are moving about this pregnancy without a fixed course may be accurate. After all, we've conditioned ourselves to believe that nothing is certain and that anything can happen along the way. Hard experience serves as the basis for this mind-set.

A secondary definition of *wandering* offered up by Merriam-Webster asserts, "to go astray." Let's ponder this idea of going astray, specifically in regard to our emotional and spiritual lives. Have you ever gone astray? Have you ever wandered off course? I certainly have. In my sin, I have wandered far from God.

I think specifically about the time when a tragedy in our family sent me into an absolute tailspin. I was eighteen years old and in my freshman year of college when my stepbrother, Chad, was killed in a car accident by a drunk driver. I had grown up with Chad as an older brother and considered him such, as his dad and my mom married when I was ten years old. Though I had surrendered my life to Jesus at the age of sixteen and had entered into a relationship with the Prince of Peace, this loss shook me to the core. I wandered far from God, initially questioning whether He even existed. My mind couldn't reconcile the injustice of it all with what I had been taught about God's character. It didn't make sense to me that the innocent died while the guilty lived. It wasn't until later that I appreciated that that's precisely what Christ did for me. When I returned to my college dorm room, after being home for a week or two with family, my roommate had taped a note on my side of our shared mirror, and in her own hand-writing it said: "'For I know the plans I have for you,' declares the Lord, 'plans to prosper you and not to harm you, plans to give you hope and a future'" (Jer. 29:11). I'll never forget those words. It wasn't until the next emotional earthquake several years later—the prenatal diagnosis of Chloe—that I turned back to God, but throughout those intervening years, He never let me go. Even though I was wandering, He remained constant, and His promises proved true.

We all do this to some degree or another. We wander off course spiritually and emotionally. As I think about the experience of pregnancy after loss, I remember how every day I wrestled with my wandering emotions. My heart longed to grieve for Chloe, who was in heaven, but it also wanted to rejoice for this baby who was yet to be born. Add in the hormonal surges, and I was an emotional roller coaster. Can you relate? Are you in a place of wandering now—spiritually or emotionally?

I've walked through several more trials since the time of my pregnancy after loss—including two more losses by miscarriage and a major marital trial. My wondering and my wandering were managed only by resting in God's promises, in His Word, and in the reality that He does have a hope and a future for me. That hope and future don't guarantee a trial-free earthly existence. Rather, by embracing the promise of the future hope He has in store—made available only through His Son Jesus—there is peace now and eternity forevermore.

peace in the promise

Therefore, since we have been justified through faith, we have peace with God through our Lord Jesus Christ, through whom we have gained access by faith into this grace in which we now stand. And we boast in the hope of the glory of God.

ROMANS 5:1–2

Embracing the Promise

You don't have to know what the future looks like because you can trust in the One who's ordained it. This is where faith comes into play. According to Scripture, "Faith is confidence in what we hope for and assurance about what we do not see" (Heb. 11:1). We need to embrace this promised hope and future now. For some, it will mean surrendering lives to Jesus for the very first time and entering into a faith in God that you've never known. In the apostle Paul's second letter to the Corinthians, he proclaimed, "Now is the time of God's favor, now is the day of salvation" (2 Cor. 6:2). I echo Paul's words; now is the time! Don't wait for the future to unfold before you place your trust in Him. Trust Him now, so that as your future unfolds—whatever the outcome—He is there to take you by the hand.

For those who've already placed their trust in Christ and who've acknowledged Jesus as Lord of their life, may the encouragement to embrace the promise be a challenge to live out your faith with great hope and a sense of peace. You will face difficult days and may be prone to wonder and to wander. In those circumstances, may you surrender to God, who holds your hope and your future in His hands.

As we trust in God by believing what His Son Jesus Christ endured for each and every one of us on the cross, there is perfect peace. We possess peace with God because our sins are forgiven, which means that we will experience eternity in heaven; what greater future hope could there be? We also experience peace in life as a result of our genuine faith, even amid difficult times. Do you truly know the Prince of Peace? I pray that you would meet with Him today.

My Pregnancy Prayer for You

Creator God, I come before You on behalf of the woman who is reading here and I pray boldly that she would understand, through the power of Your Holy Word, how intimately You know and love her. May she embrace the truth that You have a future and a hope in store for her and for the precious child that You are knitting together in her womb. Father, give her faith to believe that Your promises are true, even when feelings and circumstances try to convince her otherwise. Bring peace for this journey, Lord. Help her to embrace her future and hope in You, now. Amen.

Plans for a Future Hope

pregnancy promise ─────────────────────────

God has a future hope in store for you!

"For I know the plans I have for you," declares the LORD, "plans to prosper you and not to harm you, plans to give you hope and a future."

JEREMIAH 29:11

Lindsay was one of the first friends I told when I became pregnant with Aiyana. Together, we cofounded the Mommies with Hope ministry and were in our first year of carrying out the support group meetings for women who, like us, had experienced the loss of their babies. I remember being incredibly nervous—nervous about telling her (or anyone else for that matter), nervous about the pregnancy, nervous about whether things would truly turn out the way I hoped. Nervousness was just one of many emotions I experienced during my pregnancy with Aiyana.

Shortly after sharing my news with Lindsay, she gifted me with a treasure that now sits neatly on Aiyana's nightstand—a square, wooden plaque with the word *Hope* adorned across the top, followed by these words from the Bible: "'For I know the plans I have for you,' declares the LORD, 'plans to prosper you and not to harm you, plans to give you hope and a future'" (Jer. 29:11).

Aiyana was yet to be born, but Lindsay gave me the gift as a reminder that hope always lives. Her gift helped take my focus off of the *what ifs* regarding my pregnancy. Instead, my focus became what had always been true: God's plans for me and my precious baby who was growing within me. He has given us a future and hope, just as His Word promised.

Heavenly Father, thank You for Your perfect plan and purpose for me and my unborn child. You have a wonderfully beautiful purpose for each and every one of us, Lord, and we rest in this promise today. Help me to trust in Your plans, especially when anxiety weighs down my heart. My hope is in You, Jesus. Amen.

pen the promise ————————————————————

Do you believe that God has a future and hope for you? Journal your response and explain why you believe or doubt this truth from Scripture.

Each Day Ordained

God knows each day.

Your eyes saw my unformed body; all the days ordained for me were written in your book before one of them came to be.

PSALM 139:16

Before we saw two lines on a positive pregnancy test, heard that first murmur of a heartbeat, and long before we captured a glimpse of our little one through the technology of ultrasound, God was there. Our Creator God is weaving and knitting this little one together and has chosen the secret places of your precious body to give this tiny baby a place to grow and thrive. Each day is ordained for this precious child, just as you have been ordained to be this baby's mother. What an amazing gift to ponder.

I reflect back to my fourth pregnancy. I found out that I was pregnant just about as early as a woman possibly could. I vividly remember the joy and excitement—amidst the great trepidation—that the news of this pregnancy brought. One week later, at six weeks along in the pregnancy, I began to bleed, and it was confirmed by ultrasound and blood tests that my baby, Jesse, was gone. It was so early on that there was no "evidence" of the baby, and ultrasound revealed only an empty yolk sac. I was deeply saddened by the loss but encouraged by the truth that even though I had no tangible evidence of my baby, the Lord knew each and every one of that precious child's days. The Lord knew my child and what this baby's earthly life would entail before I could possibly know that Jesse was alive inside of me. While Jesse's existence was brief on earth, I have eternity to look forward to in heaven with this little one.

I share this story not to alarm you or cause concern, but to offer hope in the truth that while you may not be able to see the unformed body of your little one who grows within you now, you can trust that Creator God has already ordained each and every day. You can rely on God, even when you are unsure, because He knows all things. Despite the pain and sadness of our early miscarriage, I can look back and see how God was involved in every detail of Jesse's life. God is also involved in the details of your unborn child's life and you can trust that no matter the outcome, He knows each day before even one of them comes to be. He knew your yesterday, and He knows your tomorrow. In this knowing, there is great hope.

Heavenly Father, I am in awe that You have chosen me to be this baby's mother. Help me, Lord, to embrace this high calling that You have placed upon my life and to do so with faith, even when past experience and fear of loss again make it so hard. I long to know this child intimately, just as You know me and this baby You've blessed me with. Amen.

pen the promise ————————————————————

It is true that the Lord knows each day that is ordained for your child. As a mother, consider your own hopes and dreams for your child and write them down now. In prayer, surrender your list to your Sovereign God and ask Him to align your heart to His good and perfect will for your unborn child.

All Things for Good

pregnancy promise ───────────

God's plans are always for good!

And we know that in all things God works for the good of those who love him, who have been called according to his purpose.

ROMANS 8:28

I vividly recall a lunch conversation with a good friend. It was after the loss of my daughter Riyah Mae, who was now my third baby in heaven. In two years' time, I had managed to give birth to a healthy girl and then experience two miscarriages just a few months apart. My friend asked me how I was doing, and I knew she meant for me to tell her how I was *really* doing. So I told her it was hard. In my lament, I said, "I should have five children right now." My sweet friend said something in the most gentle way. "Teske," she said. "You're right. On earth, it would not be humanly possible for you to have all of your children with you. But in heaven, you have three who are already there."

We went on to talk this through, and I couldn't agree more. Because of the timing of the pregnancies and the way that they overlapped, there is no possible way that all five of my children could've been born had they survived. It pains me deeply to think about. I wish that all five of them were here with me in our little three-bedroom bungalow. But God, in His great plan and mercy, has made a way for me to one day go to them. Even now, He is working things out for my good as I continue to trust Him. He is doing the same for you, my friend.

Heavenly Father, I trust that Your plans are for good and that You are working all things together for good, even when it doesn't seem to make sense. Lord, I pray that You would help me to know and understand Your love. Help me to see Your mighty hand at work in my circumstances, even when it's difficult to look beyond the moment. In Jesus' name I pray. Amen.

pen the promise —————————————————

How have you seen God working all things together for your good? Write about it now.

Untroubled Heart

pregnancy promise ──────────────

Jesus brings comfort to a troubled heart.

"Do not let your hearts be troubled. You believe in God; believe also in me [Jesus]."

JOHN 14:1

Days are long and nights are hard when walking through life with a troubled heart. Add the physical and physiological implications of growing a whole new person in your body to the mix, and the scenario can be debilitating. When my friend Betsy was pregnant with her daughter, Layla, she struggled with believing that her daughter was going to live. Betsy had one healthy child, but since his birth, she had experienced back-to-back miscarriages. So when she became pregnant after the miscarriages, the default setting of her heart and mind was to prepare for the worst.

When Betsy was around six weeks along with Layla, she received word that hormone levels from her recent blood test didn't come back as great as hoped. This news was extremely discouraging, and she braced herself for the potential of a third miscarriage. She had to wait for a few days to retest and see if the numbers were increasing. During that period of waiting, Betsy experienced an unburdening of her understandably troubled heart. She cried incessantly in bed while a close friend came and held her. As Betsy recalled this experience, she told me, "In that moment, I just had to give this pregnancy up to God, knowing that whatever it resulted in was His plan and only He knew what would happen." As a result, she says it was "like a weight had lifted [by] putting my trust of this pregnancy in Him." I'm happy to say that Betsy's results came back positively and the pregnancy progressed normally. Layla is now almost a year old. But this doesn't mean that there weren't struggles along the way. It's a constant fight of the will to live in surrender to God and His plans. Our natural tendency is to control.

What we can learn from Betsy is that there is peace in the surrender, regardless of the outcome. God wants to carry the weight of our burdens and bring peace to our troubled hearts. Jesus Himself tells us to believe the Father and to believe also in the Son. Give your troubles over to Him today!

Dear God, please be with me as I struggle with circumstances that bring trouble to my heart. Help me, Lord, to believe in You and to believe also in Your Son Jesus, who brings great peace. Lord, please replace the troubles of my hurting and confused heart with a peace that passes understanding. I give my troubles over to You. I need your peace, Jesus! Amen.

pen the promise ————————————————

Write the troubles of your heart in your journal. In prayer, ask God to carry the weight of these burdens. As a symbol of your surrender, tear this sheet out of your journal, rip it into pieces, and discard or safely burn it.

God Can Do All Things

pregnancy promise ─────────────────────

God's purpose prevails.

"I know that you can do all things; no purpose of yours can be thwarted."

JOB 42:2

We are blessed with modern medicine, diagnostic procedures, screenings, and interventions that can be a wonderful blessing to an expectant mother. At the same time, the options can be overwhelming. Should we do this screening or not? What if an undesirable result comes back? How can we be sure if a diagnosis is accurate? These questions, and more, rise to the surface during pregnancy. Some women who've experienced a previous loss find pursuing screenings is a must, while others choose to avoid such tests. Each woman must decide for herself.

What you can know and trust in without a doubt is that God's purpose will prevail. He doesn't need a screening or a test to determine the fate of your little one because He is the creator of this child to begin with. He knows each day of this baby's life before one of them comes to be (Ps. 139:16), and He has numbered every hair upon your child's precious head (Luke 12:7). In our key verse above, Job, a righteous man who was greatly afflicted, recognizes that God's purpose ultimately prevails. It was he who said, "The LORD gave and the LORD has taken away; may the name of the LORD be praised" (Job 1:21). I ask you in all sincerity: can you echo the words of Job as you consider your own circumstances? It's difficult to give praise when all is stripped away. In the moment, it seems impossible. But with God, who can do all things, nothing is impossible.

Father in heaven, You are a good God with plans for good. Your purpose prevails, always. You can do all things, Lord. Be with me and my precious baby that I am carrying now. Bestow upon me Your favor of peace as I navigate the many care options that pregnancy presents. Guide and direct me, Lord. Help me to ultimately trust in You and Your mighty plan. Amen.

pen the promise —————————————————

As you think of your pregnancy and your history of loss, what is your reaction to Job's words in the key verse above? Write about it in your journal.

The Promise of Fearless Love

There is no fear in love. But perfect love drives out fear.

1 JOHN 4:18

Good [and Scary] News

"In one word, describe your biggest 'feeling' during pregnancy after loss," I prompted a group of women, and the responses varied. Most, if not all, shared words like *tentative, uneasy, scared, anxious, dread, nervous,* and *hesitant.* Several women cited *fear,* and while others may not have outright used that word, there was certainly a fearful undertone to their responses.

I'm guessing fear is part of your pregnancy experience, too. After all, having experienced the loss of a child prior to this pregnancy, perhaps even multiple times, we quite reasonably wonder whether it will happen again.

For many women, particularly those who haven't experienced loss, the news of pregnancy is met with great joy, excitement, and

39

anticipation. For women who've experienced loss, the news of pregnancy—even if desired, planned, and hope for—can elicit great fear and anxiety. I remember when my friend Sonya told me the news of her most recent pregnancy. She sent an email to a small group of friends that she knew would be faithful in praying for her. She started her pregnancy announcement like this:

Hello friends! I am writing to a faithful few today to share an urgent and important prayer request with you. Despite our best efforts to avoid such a situation . . . I am pregnant. We just found out last week and are still in complete shock! We are 100 percent terrified.

Sonya went on to describe her initial visit to the doctor that had taken place the week before and let us all know that she was around nine weeks along. Toward the end of her message and plea for prayer, she reiterated, "We are terrified and struggling to be positive or hang on to any hope." She indicated that they had only told a small group of people about the pregnancy and weren't sure how public they were going to make the information, especially that early on.

In this age, we've grown accustomed to seeing wonderfully creative pregnancy announcements plastered all over our Facebook news feeds. It's typically a time of excitement, rejoicing, and celebration. It certainly wasn't for Sonya, and for good reason. You see, Sonya had been on a heartbreaking journey to motherhood.

Sonya became pregnant with her first son, Elijah, only to find out midway through the pregnancy that he was developing numerous terminal complications. In addition, Sonya's life was in grave danger. After weeks of bed rest and monitoring, Elijah was not growing and his condition had not improved. Sonya had to deliver him, knowing that he would be too small to live. Elijah was born December 7, 2007, and didn't survive the birth process. It was a devastating experience and traumatized her view of pregnancy and birth.

Expecting with Hope

Soon, Sonya and her husband began talking about the possibility of adoption and attended an informational meeting through an adoption agency the following February. They went through the necessary steps, including the piles of paperwork and a home study, and began to officially "wait" for a baby to be placed with them. Miraculously, they received a call from the agency on the morning of June 3, 2008, just two months after they began to wait, informing them that they had been chosen to be the parents of a newborn baby girl, Grace. This miracle took place by the grace and providence of God, as this kind of timing is absolutely unheard of in the adoption world. They expected to be waiting at least a year. God had other plans, and the adoption of Grace was finalized in court on the one-year anniversary of precious Elijah's funeral.

Before Grace turned two, Sonya became pregnant for the second time. The doctor was optimistic about the pregnancy, and things seemed to be progressing normally. When Sonya reached thirty weeks along, she and her husband mustered up the courage to set up the crib and begin to prepare things for their new baby's arrival. Three days later, Sonya found herself in a hospital emergency room only to discover that her second baby boy, Zion, had already gone to be with Jesus. Zion was born on August 22, 2010. Devastation ensued, as Sonya dealt with the anger and pain of loss once more.

Shortly after Zion's death, Sonya was asked by a friend if they would consider adoption again, as they knew of someone arranging an adoption for a woman in prison. As the Lord would have it, the birth mother eventually agreed to meet with Sonya and her husband, and ultimately, she chose them to be the adoptive parents of her unborn baby. Sonya and her husband were able to be in the room when Zebediah was born on June 23, 2011, and they welcomed him home directly from the hospital.

By now, Sonya and her husband had decided that the prospect of having more biological children was not an option, given her painful history of loss and in accordance with the recommendation of doctors.

She continued to struggle with anger toward God, as she still longed in her heart for the ability to have her own biological child, but didn't dare try to become pregnant again. A year later, Sonya went to the doctor because she hadn't been feeling well. Despite her assurance to the doctor that she was not pregnant, a test was administered and revealed that she, in fact, was. Panic set in. It was truly a terrifying event, not because of what would be—a new baby—but because of what *could* be: the very real possibility of another loss.

peace in the promise ————————————

"So do not fear, for I am with you; do not be dismayed, for I am your God. I will strengthen you and help you; I will uphold you with my righteous right hand."

ISAIAH 41:10

You may be able to relate to Sonya's reaction. Or your initial response to the news of this pregnancy may be more welcoming. I've ministered to many women who've experienced multiple miscarriages and secondary infertility, and for them, when pregnancy finally occurs, it's a time of great joy. Still, feelings of fear and anxiety can creep in, and when they do, it's confusing. After all, we *should* be excited, right? At least that's the message we get from family and friends who just don't seem to understand the fear. When we're not excited, purely because we are scared out of our minds, guilt sneaks into the mix, and we begin brewing up a cocktail of emotional chaos that intoxicates us to the point of debilitation. Fear is the most basic ingredient in this recipe for disaster, serving as the base for so many of the other emotions that we experience during pregnancy after loss.

I remember well the constant companionship fear brought during my pregnancy with Aiyana. That fear was real and valid, and perhaps even healthy to some degree. I suspect, like me and like Sonya, that you too have welcomed fear as your friend along the journey. I'm not going to tell you that you *shouldn't* be afraid. But I will tell you that you don't *have to* be afraid. The God of all creation tells you that He is with you and He is for you; He is your God, and He will strengthen, help, and uphold you always. It is only because of His fearless love for each one of us that we have the ability to break free from the fear that holds us in bondage and keeps us from embracing the joy of the new life that is growing within us.

Understanding Love & Fear

Whether or not you have any children living, you know the fearless love of a mother. You know the overwhelming love you possess for your baby(ies) in heaven, whether you had the chance to hold or care for them on this earth or if they were born straight into Jesus' arms. Such love is so strong that it compels you to protect and to sacrifice. I imagine you would've done anything to save the life of your child, just as you would now for the one who grows within. You wouldn't think for a moment about the cost, because that's the measure of your love.

Consider this love that you have for your children and multiply that by infinity; only then can you possibly begin to grasp the fullness of God's love for you. Our peace-in-the-promise verse below tells us that God has loved us with an everlasting love; He's drawn us to Himself with unfailing kindness. Eternity past, to eternity future. That's how much God loves you, me, and each of our precious children. No human love can quite compare with the depth of God's supernatural love for humanity.

peace in the promise ————————————————————

"I have loved you with an everlasting love; I have drawn you with unfailing kindness."

JEREMIAH 31:3

There is much to be said about love in God's Word. We can read entire volumes of books written solely on the topic of God's love. Jesus tells us that the greatest command is to "love the Lord your God with all your heart and with all your soul and with all your strength and with all your mind" and goes on to say that the second greatest commandment is to "love your neighbor as yourself" (Luke 10:27). One of the most well-known verses in Scripture says, "For God so loved the world that he gave his one and only Son, that whoever believes in him shall not perish but have eternal life" (John 3:16). First John 3:16 defines love by asserting, "This is how we know what love is: Jesus Christ laid down his life for us." The love of God for us is sacrificial. So much so, that He gave His only Son.

God's Fearless Love for You

We started this chapter out with our peace-in-the-promise verse from 1 John 4:18, which states, "There is no fear in love. But perfect love drives out fear." That verse goes on to say, "Because fear has to do with punishment. The one who fears is not made perfect in love." As we apply this verse to our fear during pregnancy after loss, let's read it in the context of the verses around it to make sure we clearly understand what is being said:

Dear friends, let us love one another, for love comes from God. Everyone who loves has been born of God and knows God. Whoever does not love does not know God, because God is love. This is how God showed his love among us: He sent his one and only Son into the world that we might live through him. This is love: not that we loved God, but that he loved us and sent his Son as an atoning sacrifice for our sins. Dear friends, since God so loved us, we also ought to love one another. No one has ever seen God; but if we love one another, God lives in us and his love is made complete in us.

This is how we know that we live in him and he in us: He

has given us of his Spirit. And we have seen and testify that the Father has sent his Son to be the Savior of the world. If anyone acknowledges that Jesus is the Son of God, God lives in them and they in God. And so we know and rely on the love God has for us.

God is love. Whoever lives in love lives in God, and God in them. This is how love is made complete among us so that we will have confidence on the day of judgment: In this world we are like Jesus. There is no fear in love. But perfect love drives out fear, because fear has to do with punishment. The one who fears is not made perfect in love. We love because he first loved us." (1 John 4:7–19)

As we examine these verses, we find that the word *love* or some variation of it is stated twenty-two times in thirteen verses. Apparently, God has something to teach us about love in this short passage of Scripture. When we look at the original Greek language, we find that the Greek word *agape* (or some variation of this, depending on tense) is the word used in every instance. Knowing this helps us to better understand the nature of the passage and God's agape love for each and every one of us. *Agape* is the same Greek word that is used in John 3:16: "For God so loved (*agapao*) the world." Agape love refers to the sacrificial love that God has for us, His creation, made evident through the cross of Jesus Christ.

Such love is so overwhelming and absolutely mind-boggling, that it can give us the power to live our lives with great faith and trust in the lover of our souls. If you've acted on faith before, you know exactly what I mean. Consider the earlier loss of your child or children. I imagine you may sometimes look back and ask, how did I ever make it through? As I ponder my own losses, I can't help but wonder the same. Yet it doesn't take me long to conclude that it was only by the supernatural love and grace of God made known through Jesus. Because of His great and fearless love, we can face all things in life with confidence.

This confidence has absolutely nothing to do with any foresight that we'll obtain our desired circumstances. It has everything to do with knowing who we are in Him. The Scripture passage above conveys to us a message of great hope in affirming that if we have Jesus in our hearts—if we've met the Prince of Peace—there is no need to fear. We need not fear judgment when we face Him (v. 17) because we already belong to Him. We need not fear trials, because He's already overcome. We can experience peace in the promise of God's fearless love because of who He is and who we are in Him. Sure, there is a place for a healthy fear of the Lord. But this is entirely different from fretting over our circumstances.

peace in the promise

The fear of the LORD leads to life; then one rests content, untouched by trouble.

PROVERBS 19:23

Fear of the Lord Doesn't Mean to Be Afraid

Let me be clear: fear of the Lord does not mean that we should be afraid of God. This is an important distinction to make. Fear of the Lord leads to life, satisfaction, and rest. Psalm 111:10 says, "The fear of the LORD is the beginning of wisdom." The precise phrase, "fear of the Lord," is found more than twenty times in Scripture. Many of these references point to the truth that fear of the Lord has to do with wisdom, understanding, and knowledge of God (Job 28:28; Ps. 111:10; Prov. 1:7; 2:5; 9:10). Several verses from the prophet Isaiah point to Jesus when sharing about the fear of the Lord. For example, Isaiah 11 begins, "A shoot will come up from the stump of Jesse; from his roots a Branch will bear fruit" (v. 1). Isaiah was prophesying about Jesus, the Branch, referring back to His lineage through Jesse, the father of King David. Isaiah went on to describe Jesus in the following manner:

The Spirit of the LORD will rest on him—the Spirit of wisdom and of understanding, the Spirit of counsel and of might, the Spirit of the knowledge and fear of the LORD—and he will delight in the fear of the LORD. (vv. 2–3)

Jesus Himself is described in Scripture as one who possesses fear of the Lord. What's more, He delights in the fear of the Lord; a true example for how we ought to live. Living life with a delightful fear of the Lord is the only fear we ought to have. After all, it is He who makes the path straight (Prov. 3:6), He who gives wisdom and understanding (Prov. 2:6), and He who spoke creation into its very existence (Gen. 1; John 1:1). So let us revere God, not be afraid of Him. When we possess a healthy fear—fear of the Lord—we are honoring God, realizing our need to be saved from the mess of our sinful selves, and relying on Him to bring wisdom, knowledge, and understanding.

peace in the promise ————————————————————

For God gave us a spirit not of fear but of power and love and self-control.

2 TIMOTHY 1:7 ESV

Breaking Free from Fear

This all sounds good, but what does it look like to break free from the fear that is keeping me in bondage? How can I rest, satisfied in God, and keep this unhealthy fear from consuming my every thought and action?

Believe, surrender, trust, and keep the faith. It starts here. There's no magic formula to wash away the fear. Rather, it's a continual process that takes discipline and obedience. Love, as we've learned, requires action. When we act in love, we are being intentional. Our faith is a response to God's love for us. "We love because he first loved us" (1 John 4:19). So, when feelings of fear creep in, we must remember what we believe, surrender those feelings of fear over to the Lord, and trust that He has our best interest at heart. Throughout your pregnancy, there will be times of fear and anxiety. There will also be moments of relief. My desire for you is that through it all, peace would underpin every emotion. This is possible not because of any guarantee from me but because you have the ability to let God's fearless love be your guide. If you've met Jesus, the Prince of Peace, and He lives in your heart, then you have the ability to break free from the fear that holds you captive.

Here are some practical ways to address fear during your pregnancy:

- *Take Inventory.* What fears are you currently struggling with about your pregnancy? Put a label on your fears so that you can deliberately and specifically bring them to God in prayer.
- *Examine.* Take some time to assess the situation by asking yourself some tough questions. Pray for God to bring an honest appraisal to light and to give you the strength to bear the answers, because quite honestly, the truth may sting. Are these fears rational? What lies do I believe that contribute to my fears? Are these fears consuming me (my time, my relationships, my walk with God)? Are these fears ruling me (idolatry)?
- *Confess and Repent.* In examining yourself, issues may surface that require you to confess and repent. If you've identified lies and irrational beliefs, arm yourself with Truth to replace the lie. Memorize Scripture. Start with the peace-in-the-promise verses shared throughout this chapter. Write them on note cards and place them in strategic places in your home, office, or vehicle. If fear is consuming you and becoming an idol in your life, confess this sin to God and repent—turn away from the sin and look to God. Ask Him to order your steps, occupy your thoughts, and help you to see when fear creeps in and threatens to take over. Place Jesus back on the throne of your heart and kick fear to the curb.

Expecting with Hope

- *Stay Surrendered.* Once you've replaced lies with truth, and confessed and repented from sin, it is absolutely essential that you stay surrendered. You've laid this all at Jesus' feet—leave it there. When you are tempted to pick the fear back up, don't give in. You can do this.

Some element of fear will undoubtedly be part of this pregnancy journey. But fear does not have to be your constant companion. It is my prayer that the supernatural, fearless love of God will drive out any fears that hold you captive. May you continually trust in Him.

Sonya's Super Silas

You may be wondering about Sonya and how her story turned out. It wasn't an easy road, by any means, but it was certainly miraculous. If you haven't figured it out by now, God doesn't call us to "easy." So often, however, those miracles in our lives that are absolutely the most beautiful are only so because of the difficult journey that got us there. Such was the case in Sonya's story.

On January 30, 2013, when she was thirty weeks along, Sonya gave birth to a precious little boy, Silas . . . who was alive! Given Sonya's history, she received very close monitoring throughout her pregnancy, and the plan from the beginning was that she would deliver this baby at thirty weeks. The risk of her carrying him to term was greater than the alternative of him being born early and cared for in the neonatal intensive care unit (NICU). In a testimony that Sonya gave at her local church on Mother's Day this past year, she recalled the pregnancy this way: "After everything we've been through, those thirty weeks were the hardest weeks of my life. Every day was filled with fear, and we were too afraid to hold on to hope." Despite all fear, Silas was born living and thriving. After five-and-a-half weeks in the NICU, he was discharged to go home, healthy. As I write these words, Sonya and her husband are making plans for a "Super Sy" first-birthday celebration.

Sonya vulnerably shared her story, giving God honor and praise

Sonya's Super Silas
(Photo by Destri Andorf of d&orfs photography. Used with permission.)

along the way. While trusting Him was hard, she learned some lessons along her journey that I believe each of us needs to hear and embrace. Sonya so eloquently reported:

"I have learned how fragile life is. Things can change in the blink of an eye, and all we can cling to is Jesus. I have learned the value of fellowship. We would not have made it through those dark times without the support and prayers of friends and family. I have learned to trust that God works for good, even in the darkest times. Whether you can find hope or not, it is there, and good will prevail."

Yes, and amen!

My Pregnancy Prayer for You

Father, thank You for Your fearless love for each and every one of us. Thank You for loving us so much that You gave Your only Son Jesus. It is because of Your great love, His willing sacrifice, and Your mighty power that raised Him from the dead that we are able to live a life of peace. I pray for this woman who reads here now, Lord, that You would overflow her heart with a sense of Your amazing, unfailing, fearless love found in Christ Jesus. May she respond with praise and thanksgiving. Instill in her a peace that surpasses human understanding as Your truth permeates her every thought. Take every bit of worry and fear and transform it into a prayer of surrender. All these things I pray in the saving love of Jesus. Amen.

Expecting with Hope

A Fearless Love

pregnancy promise ———————————————————

True love is fearless.

There is no fear in love. But perfect love drives out fear, because fear has to do with punishment. The one who fears is not made perfect in love.

1 JOHN 4:18

I'd be lying if I told you that, through all of my pregnancies after Chloe died, I was able to walk in complete faith and without fear. I was paralyzed with fear at times, and I often wondered if my journey was some sort of punishment for baggage that I was holding on to from the birth of my first child. I was unmarried and eighteen years old when I became pregnant with Gabe, who was born happy and healthy. I struggled with postpartum depression but refused to get help, and quite honestly I didn't feel like I was a good mother at all. In my mind, surely those were the reasons we lost Chloe. So why would God consider blessing a broken woman like me?

It took time and truth for me to discover the many lies and the fear that were at the root of these horrible thoughts of punishment. The truth is, God is love (1 John 4:8) and in Him there is no darkness (1 John 1:5). The dark cloud of fear, doubt, and punishment was self-inflicted and didn't represent God's heart toward me or any one of my children. Rather, He had chosen me to be the mother for each of my children. I was and am blessed to have two miracles on earth as well as my three precious babies in heaven.

Once I was able to grasp the mind-blowing, lavish love and grace of God, I was able to love my children without fear that I would fail them—in the womb while carrying them, and on this earth as I raise them. God poured out His fearless love for me, for you, and for the babies He's entrusted to our care. He gave it all, without fear, on the cross.

Father in heaven, You are love. We love only because You first loved us. Thank You, Lord, for demonstrating such fearless love for me on the cross. Help me to know the great and wondrous love that You have for me and for my child that I carry within. Bring Your truth, Lord, to weed out every lie I've believed and every accusation from the Enemy. Drive out my fears with Your perfect love, Lord Jesus. Amen.

pen the promise

What is your view of God's love for you? Has your loss and pregnancy experiences shaped how you view God's love for you?

When Anxiety Is Great

pregnancy promise ————————————————————

God's consolation brings joy.

When anxiety was great within me, your consolation brought me joy.

PSALM 94:19

There will be times along this journey when you feel tremendous anxiety. Your concerns are real, and they are valid. Countless questions are now part of an experience that was once so innocent and so welcomed. Now you wonder, what are my hCG levels? Should I be taking progesterone? Will I make it past _____ weeks? What if there's a prenatal diagnosis? Why can't I feel the baby move yet? Why don't I have more severe symptoms? The list goes on and on. When questions consume, and anxiety overwhelms, we can become paralyzed.

The truth is, worry and anxiety will only serve to add undue stress to your pregnancy. As the psalmist wrote in our key verse above, the consolation of God brings joy. Yes, even when anxiety is great, joy is available. Joy is possible. You have to be willing to give your cares to Him. Think now of your greatest fear or worry. In prayer, give it over to God and ask Him to bring consolation to your worried soul. The Lord is faithful to be found as you seek Him with your whole heart. In doing so, there is great joy, even amid the uncertainty.

Dear God, There are times on this journey of pregnancy after loss when anxiety is overwhelming and paralyzing. Lord, I ask that You would bring consolation and joy to my anxious heart. I have many questions and cares that I need to cast upon You. Help me, Lord. Please work within my heart and spirit so that I may surrender these cares to You. Replace every one of my irrational thoughts and every worrisome fear with thoughts of Your fearless love, and console my hurting heart. In the powerful name of Jesus, I pray. Amen.

pen the promise —————————————————

What makes you most anxious at this time? How can you let God console you?

Expecting with Hope

Cast Your Cares . . . And Leave Them

pregnancy promise ——————————————

God cares for you and wants to carry your burdens.
Cast all your anxiety on him because he cares for you.

1 PETER 5:7

In recent months, I had a conversation with a friend about the issue of casting our cares upon the Lord. Both of us had various concerns that were weighing heavily on our hearts—family matters, financial struggles, an impending move, job changes, and the like. We shared our hearts with one another, revealing what the Lord was teaching us as we walked through these challenging circumstances.

My friend expressed that she was really good about giving Jesus her worries, but that she was also really good about picking them back up. We chuckled for a moment but went on to discuss how serious of a challenge this can be. She asked me to hold her accountable and gave me permission to ask her if she's leaving her worries with Jesus or if she's picking them back up.

This conversation has stuck with me as I've pondered the many worries that I so freely give over to the Lord, only to pick them up again. I imagine that you can relate to this, too. The worries and anxieties that women wrestle with during pregnancy after loss are ones that we seem to hold on to tightly. The verse above encourages and reminds us that God cares for us and wants us to cast our cares upon Him. And to leave them in His very capable hands.

Father in heaven, thank You for caring for me so much that You would instruct me to cast my cares upon You. During this pregnancy, my cares are many, Lord. I give them to You now. Help me, Jesus, to leave these worries at Your feet, and give me the strength to walk forward with a holy confidence in You alone. Amen.

pen the promise ────────────────

What cares do you need to cast on Jesus today? Write them in your journal and give them over to Him in prayer. Remember, don't pick them back up!

That's the Spirit

pregnancy promise ────────────────────

God gives us a spirit of power, love, and self-control.
God gave us a spirit not of fear but of power and love and self-control.

2 TIMOTHY 1:7 ESV

What do you think your husband would say if I were to ask him, In one word how would you describe your wife's spirit during this pregnancy? If someone were to ask my husband that during my pregnancy days, he might have been afraid to answer honestly. He may have said, "excited," but been truly thinking, "One word? How about a few choice words—crazy, basket case, nervous wreck." I know he wouldn't have been able to say my spirit was powerful, loving, or exuding self-control.

Yet these are the descriptive words used in our key verse above. We are told that God gives us a spirit *not of fear*, but of power, love, and self-control. This, my friends, is a game changer. You don't have to be fearful, because by God's power, you can think, respond, and react differently as you journey through this pregnancy. You are free to love this child without fear, because God gives you the strength. You can exert power over your emotions and exert self-control when you feel out of control, because of the power of the Holy Spirit. For the follower of Jesus, the Holy Spirit indwells your very heart, and thereby gives you the power to bear the fruit of the Spirit; love, joy, peace, forbearance, kindness, goodness, faithfulness, gentleness, and self-control (Gal. 5:22–23). Breathe a sigh of relief, relinquish the spirit of fear, and put on the fruit of the Spirit!

Dear God, Thank You for giving us a spirit, not of fear, but of love.

Help this precious woman who reads here now to embrace Your love. May her response to You generate fruit in her attitude and life that reflect the powerful work of the Holy Spirit inside of her. Give her forbearance, peace, gentleness, and self-control as she navigates the many tough emotions of grief and joy intertwined. Amen.

pen the promise ———————————————————

In one word, how would you describe your current spirit during this pregnancy? If necessary, what practical steps can you take to embrace a spirit of love, as described in our key verse above?

Called You By Name

The Lord calls you by name.

"Do not fear, for I have redeemed you; I have summoned you by name; you are mine."

ISAIAH 43:1

Finding out the gender of our baby during my pregnancy after loss was a turning point for me. Discovering that we were expecting a daughter gave me permission, in a way, to bond with her as she grew within. Together, my husband and I chose her name—*Aiyana Elise*, which means "forever flowering" and "oath of God." We spent the next weeks and months getting to know our girl, calling her by name.

Whether we would have chosen a name for her during pregnancy or not, we can rest in the truth that God knew her by name. He knows each one of us by name. Scripture tells us that He even knows the number of hairs that grace our heads (Luke 12:7). He, too, knows your baby by name. What's more, He doesn't merely know us, He summons us. He calls us to Himself, and we are His.

What about our babies who are with Him in heaven? Yes, He knows them, too, more intimately than we can fathom, whether we've named them or not. What matters most is that God has called them by name; He calls us by name. He is our Redeemer, and He summons each one of us into a deeper relationship with Him. As you walk through the remainder of this pregnancy, consider how God is calling you by name.

Father in heaven, You know me by name. You know my children by name—my baby(ies) in heaven with You now, and my baby who grows within. Help me, Lord, to trust Your Word and the promises it contains. Thank You for being my Redeemer and my King. Help me to grow in my relationship with You, Lord Jesus. Amen.

pen the promise —————————————————————

How is God beckoning you into closer relationship with Him?

Expecting with Hope

The Promise of His Presence

peace in the promise —————————————————————

"Be strong and courageous. Do not be afraid or terrified because of them, for the LORD your God goes with you; he will never leave you nor forsake you."

DEUTERONOMY 31:6

The presence of God brings great peace. Think of examples from your own life. Can you recall a time when you've felt the very real presence of God and been overwhelmed by an unbelievable sense of peace? As I reflect upon my own answer to that question, a couple of situations come to mind right away, each of which tends to be in the center or aftermath of some major trial. I have to admit that in my everyday life I often take God's presence and the peace He brings for granted. Too often I don't live as though I truly believe that He is with me, within me, for me, and before me. God is all these things simply and *only* because Jesus entered the earth as a baby Himself, for me. He came for you, too, my friend.

As we delve into a deeper understanding of this promise, we are going to examine God's presence in two ways: (1) God is everywhere, and (2) God is within. The former is a universal truth, meaning it applies to everyone. The latter is a truth for those who *know* Him, who've made peace with God through the Prince of Peace—Jesus— by trusting in His finished work on the cross. But before He made His way to the cross, He had to make His way into our world. The first chapter of the gospel of John tells us clearly, "the Word [Jesus] became flesh and made his dwelling among us" (v. 14). It is my great hope that you are able to experience God's presence in both of these ways—everywhere *and* within, but only because of the good news that Jesus came to save.

Everywhere

At the beginning of this book, we dove into several verses from Psalm 139 as we worked to gain an understanding of God's intimate knowledge of and love for each and every one of us. What we didn't spend a whole lot of time focusing on was the reality of His presence, as is so clearly evident throughout that passage of Scripture. In Psalm 139, the psalmist poses a series of questions to God and provides an immediate answer to each:

> Where can I go from your Spirit?
>> Where can I flee from your presence?
> If I go up to the heavens, you are there;
>> if I make my bed in the depths, you are there.
> If I rise on the wings of the dawn,
>> if I settle on the far side of the sea,
> even there your hand will guide me,
>> your right hand will hold me fast. (vv. 7–10)

With confidence, the psalmist tells of God's presence *everywhere* he goes. Likewise, God is everywhere you and I go. He's with you during every doctor's appointment, in the dark of every worry-filled night, and in the light of every joy-filled flutter. He is even in the secret place of your womb where He continues to knit your precious baby together now (Ps. 139:13–16).

Isaiah 30:21 says, "Whether you turn to the right or to the left, your ears will hear a voice behind you, saying, 'This is the way; walk in it.'" Consider the encouraging visual that this verse provides. Whichever way you go, God is with you. He's right behind you. Psalm 23:6 affirms this illustration by stating, "surely your goodness and love will *follow* me all the days of my life" (emphasis added). He *is* goodness and mercy. And when we seem to get off course, He brings us back because of His goodness and mercy. Proverbs 3:6 tells us plainly that "He will make your paths straight" as you trust in Him. Our sovereign God goes before you and He follows after you. He knows the outcome of this pregnancy, and He is already there, my friend.

God is with us now as we meet here within the pages of this book. In Scripture, Jesus tells us, "For where two or three gather in my name, there am I with them" (Matt. 18:20). As I write these words, I am calling upon the mighty and powerful name of Jesus to meet with us here as we seek to understand the very great and precious promises of His Word that will lead you to a place of peace amid your pregnancy. With Jesus, we can trust that no matter the outcome, He will be with us through it all. He's been faithful in the past, He is faithful in our present, and we can trust Him to be faithful in our future because Jesus reigns supreme. Paul's letter to the Colossians describes Jesus like this:

The Son is the image of the invisible God, the firstborn over all creation. For in him all things were created: things in heaven and on earth, visible and invisible, whether thrones or powers or rulers or authorities; all things have been created through him and for him. He is before all things, and in him all things hold together. And he is the head of the body, the church; he is the beginning and the firstborn from among the dead, so that in everything he might have the supremacy. For God was pleased to have all his fullness dwell in him, and through him to reconcile to himself all things, whether things on earth or things in heaven, by making peace through his blood, shed on the cross. (Col. 1:15–20)

Let's not overlook the powerful truths contained in this passage of Scripture. We learn that Jesus is the image of the invisible God; God in the flesh. He was born into the world, fully human and fully God. Through Jesus' sacrifice on the cross, we are reconciled to God to experience peace, fellowship, and joy forevermore.

Within

If you've trusted in Jesus as your Savior, then the Holy Spirit indwells your very heart (1 Cor. 3:16; 6:19–20). He lives within you. Thus, God's presence is always with you and within you. This is an especially comforting truth for those times when anxiety threatens to rule our hearts and worst-case scenarios invade our minds.

As we acknowledge God's presence within, as a result of truly knowing Jesus, we must acknowledge the promise of His fearless love. If it were not for His love, a love displayed by the sacrifice Jesus made on the cross, then it wouldn't be possible to have the Holy Spirit living within. Once we know Him, however—really *know* Him—absolutely nothing can separate us from His love. Paul's letter to the Romans assures us of this:

For I am sure that neither death nor life, nor angels nor rulers, nor things present nor things to come, nor powers, nor height nor depth, nor anything else in all creation, will be able to separate us from the love of God in Christ Jesus our Lord." (Romans 8:38–39 ESV)

Nothing can separate you—or me, or anyone else who knows the Prince of Peace—from the love of God that is found in Jesus.

Expecting with Hope

He Made His Dwelling Among Us

This Jesus, our Prince of Peace, is the One who brings perfect peace. But that's only possible because He came to earth and made His dwelling among us. To think that the God of all creation entered in to the brokenness of this world to rescue us is absolutely astounding. We tend to lose our sense of awe and wonder over this miraculous truth.

We all know the story of Jesus' birth: conceived by the Holy Spirit, born of the virgin Mary, no room at the inn, and therefore born in a manger. We've heard or told the story so many times that it may seem common and ordinary. At Christmastime, we see lawns and mantles adorned with nativity scenes, depicting the story of old. We sing carols and hymns that reflect upon the account. It's all so familiar, both for those who grew up in church with the things of God and those who did not. And you know what? There's absolutely nothing common or ordinary about it. The story is positively divine from beginning to end.

John 1:1 explains, "In the beginning was the Word, and the Word was with God, and the Word was God." Later in the chapter we read that "the Word became flesh and made his dwelling among us" (v. 14). What? you may ask. How is the "Word" a "He"? Simply stated, because He is the Word. The remainder of the verse goes on to say, "We have seen his glory, the glory of the one and only Son, who came from the Father, full of grace and truth." Yes, the Word is the Son: precious Jesus. He has existed from the beginning, but at a strategic moment in time, He chose to come to earth as a baby born in a manger to grow into a man who would die on a cross.

Consider your own pregnancy for a moment. Whether you've done any preparation or not, you have to admit that some degree of planning must go into effect the closer you get to giving birth: diapers, supplies, car seat, crib. There may even be a baby shower held in your honor, hosted by eager (and borderline obnoxious, overly excited) family and friends. You may fall on either end of the spectrum in terms of your outlook on all this planning; anywhere from totally disengaged, perhaps as an attempt to protect yourself from the potential hurt of another loss, to overly consumed by the pregnancy and preparations as a way to ensure that everything will be done "just right" this time. Whatever the case, we can all agree that some degree of planning must take place before baby arrives. The planning and preparing is all well and good, but let us be careful not to get so disengaged or over-engaged that we fail to neglect the *miracle* of this marvelous creation.

By disengaging, we deny the very real presence of our child who grows within. This is usually an attempt to guard our hearts from the potential pain of another loss. The problem with this approach is that we let fear rule. Quite honestly, whether you admit it or not, you've already connected to your baby by the mere fact that you know you're pregnant. If you didn't care for the child, you wouldn't fear the potential loss and wouldn't try to disengage. In contrast, by over-engaging, we run the risk of allowing the baby, activities, tasks, and lists to take over and consume. When we are *consumed* by anything, we ought to ask if that person, activity, or thing has kicked Jesus off the throne of our hearts. He should always take center stage. Through it all, we must bear in mind the very real and present help of Jesus, who came and made His dwelling among us by miraculously entering the world as a baby Himself.

peace in the promise ————————————

God is our refuge and strength, an ever-present help in trouble.

PSALM 46:1

Ever-Present Help

This peace-in-the-promise verse tells us plainly that God is an ever-present help in trouble. Other translations explain that God is "always ready to help" (NLT) or "a very present help" (NASB). The psalm goes on to describe some of the trouble, by stating:

Therefore we will not fear, though the earth give way and the mountains fall into the heart of the sea, though its waters roar and foam and the mountains quake with their surging. . . . The LORD Almighty is with us; the God of Jacob is our fortress. (Ps. 46:2–3, 7)

The very present help of God brings security to the psalmist. Just as God was a very real and present help to him, He desires to be our help. Whether the world is crumbling around us after loss, or we find ourselves on top of the mountain in a season of great joy and blessing, He is there. We don't have to fear, because we can trust in the ever-present nature of our wonderful God.

Our peace-in-the-promise verse that began this chapter comes from a passage in Deuteronomy. The verse commands: "Be strong and courageous. Do not be afraid or terrified . . . ; he will never leave you nor forsake you" (Deut. 31:6). It's helpful to understand the context of these verses so that we know who is telling whom not to fear and that God is with them. In Deuteronomy 31, Moses is passing the torch to Joshua, charging him with the task of leading the Israelites to the Promised Land. After all, Moses tells the people, "I am now a hundred and twenty years old and I am no longer able to lead you" (v. 2). The Lord had made it known to Moses that Joshua was the man to lead the Israelites across the Jordan River, instructing Moses not to cross. Moses explained this changing of the guard to the Israelites, assuring them of their safety because of the Lord's guidance and presence. Then Moses directly told Joshua to "be strong and courageous" (v. 7), going on to repeat the same message that he had just shared with the Israelites: "The LORD himself goes before you and will be with you; he will never leave you nor forsake you. Do not be afraid; do not be discouraged" (v. 8).

In context, these words were a promise from God to the Israelites and to their newly appointed leader, Joshua. We see these same words in the New Testament book of Hebrews, which is noted for the many Old Testament quotations that appear throughout the text. This is precisely what the writer does in Hebrews 13:5, which reads, "Keep your lives free from the love of money and be content with what you have, because God has said, 'Never will I leave you; never will I forsake you.'" He has applied this promise—original to the Israelites and to Joshua—to us all. The writer then goes on to quote another Old Testament passage (Ps. 118:6–7), which says, "The Lord is my helper; I will not be afraid. What can mere mortals do to me?" (Heb. 13:6). In Scripture, we find that these promises are more widely applied to each and every one of us. He is with us, He is for us, He was before us, and He goes before us. We don't have to be afraid because of the very real and present help of our great God.

peace in the promise ───────────────

The eyes of the LORD are in every place, keeping watch on the evil and the good.

PROVERBS 15:3 ESV

Squarely in His Sight

There will be times throughout this pregnancy and well after this baby is born when fear and worry creep back in. I can vividly recall a time when fear sent me into a tailspin in a matter of minutes as I feared for the well-being of my then ten-year-old son, Gabe. The sound of a car horn captured my attention as I sat in the quietness of my kitchen one fall afternoon. I lifted my head and peered across the house, through the living room, and out the front-door window to notice my fifth-grade son's bike laying on the ground in our front yard. It was just after three o'clock, but he hadn't come in the door from his routine bike ride home from school. A few seconds passed, and suddenly my heart dropped as I wondered if the car horn had something to do with *why* my son hadn't walked through the door. Had he been hit?

I jumped to my feet and hurried to the front of the house. Gabe was nowhere in sight. I walked outside, peered around the garage, and walked down both sides of the house. He was gone. Heart pounding, I ran inside calling for him, "Gabe? Gaaabe?" Surely, he must have come in and raced off to the bathroom or something. Up and down the stairs, in and out of every room, I called out his name. I felt as though the search for him lasted an hour, when in all actuality, only a few minutes had gone by. All the while, fears of abduction filled my thoughts with visions of making a dreadful 911 call and the burden of having to tell my husband. These thoughts ran rampant as I continued to yell for him.

Finally, I heard him faintly through the screen of our deck door on the back side of our house. "Yeah. Why are you yelling?" By his tone, I can sense that he wondered what kind of craziness had overcome his mother that she would be yelling his name throughout the house for the neighborhood to hear. What a great relief to hear and then see Gabe— alive and well. He was walking on the sidewalk just south of our corner home. As I made my way onto our back deck, I asked with concern:

"Where were you?"

Matter-of-factly, he replied: "I was walking [home from school]."

"Why is your bike out front?" I questioned.

"Luke hurt his leg today, so I offered to let him ride my bike so he could get home quicker."

My heart melted, and tears welled up as I realized exactly what was going on. Gabe, who typically rides his bike to and from school, lent his bike to his hurting classmate who lives just a bit farther down the road. That's why it took him longer to get home while his bike lay abandoned in the front yard. The car horn? No explanation, but there were certainly no candy-luring abductions taking place in my neighborhood that afternoon.

It's amazing how quickly our minds can jump to the worst-case scenario. This afterschool ordeal caused me to pause and remember that God had Gabe squarely in His sights all along. And guess what? He would've been with him—with me—even if my worst nightmare had come true. He loves him more than I could ever imagine, yet He entrusts me to be his mother: a mother who teaches him to love and to "be a light," our daily mantra when sending him off into the world. And that's precisely what he did that day by showing love to a friend in need. He sacrificed his own comfort and thought nothing of it—all the while showing me a simple picture of love in action.

It's a precious gift to bear the responsibility of raising a son *for* the Son; the gift multiplies when you see your son living out Jesus' command to love our neighbor. Yes, our minds wander and our mommy hearts worry, but the unfailing, fearless love of the Father remains. Amid every worry and fear that we face during pregnancy and motherhood, we can rely on the faithful presence of the Lord. As Psalm 145:18 says, "The LORD is near to all who call on him, to all who call on him in truth." God has not made a mistake in choosing you to be this baby's mother. May you rest in the presence and promise of His fearless love now, as you wait for your child to enter this world, and on into tomorrow when his or her precious life continues to teach you what it means to continually rely on the Father's presence. Call on Him. He is an ever-present help (Ps. 46:1).

My Pregnancy Prayer for You

Dear Lord, thank You for being an ever-present God. You see all, You know all, and You are with us through it all. For those of us who know You, God, Your magnificent Holy Spirit dwells within. Help us to live our lives in full knowledge and comprehension that our bodies are temples of Your Holy Spirit. Heavenly Father, I pray for the woman who reads here now and ask that You would make Your marvelous presence known to her in the most intimate of ways. If she has not entered into a relationship with You through Jesus, I pray today would be the day of salvation. If she already knows You as Lord of her life, I pray that her faith would be refreshed and revived as Your presence penetrates every aspect of her life! Thank You for loving us so much that You choose to be with us through it all. In Jesus' name we pray. Amen.

Expecting with Hope

Be Strong and Courageous

pregnancy promise ────────────────

The Lord God is with you.

"Have I not commanded you? Be strong and courageous. Do not be afraid; do not be discouraged, for the LORD your God will be with you wherever you go."

JOSHUA 1:9

Some things are easier said than done, right? After all, it's one thing to tell somebody else to "be strong and courageous" and it's another thing to live out this command on one's own. Fear and anxiety are common emotions experienced by women who become pregnant after miscarriage, stillbirth, or infant loss. I remember the mix of emotions that enveloped me when I first found out I was pregnant a year after Chloe died. To say I was scared is an understatement. What if this child had some rare genetic disorder, too? I know the doctor said that it was a "random mix-up of the genes" and that the chances of something like this happening again were "slim to none." But still.

I didn't keep my emotions in check and, quite honestly, was a basket case at times. Yet I had hope. Not because of medical certainties or scientific rationale. My hope came from a faith in the God who promised me that He would be with me wherever I went. My God commanded me to "be strong and courageous," but He didn't leave me to do so on my own. Rather, He assured me that He would be walking alongside me on this journey. What a relief. Did you know He longs to walk with you, too? Indeed, He is with you today and will be with you in the days to come. Take this truth to heart and take courage, fellow mommy.

Heavenly Father, I know You tell us not to be afraid, but I admit, Lord, I am. Please wrap Your loving, faithful arms around me now and help me to see Your overwhelming presence in my life. Give me the strength to be strong and courageous, Lord, as You have commanded. Help me to experience Your ever-present help and encouragement as I continue to carry this child who grows within. In the name of Jesus, I pray. Amen.

pen the promise ——————————————————

What are your fears about this pregnancy? Write them in your journal. Pray and ask God to bring peace to your heart with regard to these fears.

Expecting with Hope

Always with Me

pregnancy promise ————————————————

God knows you intimately and is with you wherever you go.
Where can I go from your Spirit? Where can I flee from your presence?

PSALM 139:7

You can try to flee from God, but you won't get very far. Trust me, I've tried. When I was eighteen, my stepbrother was killed by a drunk driver. It was my first significant grief experience and it sent me into a sea of questions, deep grief, and anger. I ran from the Lord, turned my back on Him, and questioned, "If God is good, then why did my stepbrother have to die?" It was a dark and difficult time, marked by many sleepless nights. Nightmares kept me awake, afraid. So in my rebellion I partied through the nights and slept through my days.

Years later, after I had settled down and come to terms with the loss, I was rocked by the news of Chloe's diagnosis and terminal prognosis. I faced a fork in the road. I could travel down that lonely path of desperation once again, or run straight toward my God, who in all actuality had never let me go. He had been with me all along, but I refused to let Him in. The Lord says, "Who can hide in secret places so that I cannot see them? . . . Do not I fill heaven and earth?" (Jer. 23:24).

He has been with me in those seasons of grief, just as surely as He has carried me through seasons of blessing. He's always present, incredibly real, and forever faithful. He is gracious and compassionate, steadfast and merciful. Though I had run far from Him, I couldn't outrun His love and mercy, made evident by how He so graciously welcomed me back into His arms. He was and is always with me. He's with you always, too, friend. Press in all the more closely to Him today.

Dear God, thank You for being a God who never lets His children go. You are so faithful, Lord, and I am forever grateful for Your mercy. Help me rest in the open arms of Your embrace and to truly believe that You are with me, even when I don't feel Your presence. Make Your presence known to me so that I may experience Your love in a deep and soul-changing way today. In the precious name of Jesus. Amen.

pen the promise

Have you ever tried to run from God? Write about that experience in your journal.

My Ever-Present Help

pregnancy promise ————————————————————

God is there to help you.

God is our refuge and strength, an ever-present help in trouble.

PSALM 46:1

You may be familiar with this key verse. It's one that many Christians turn to or share for encouragement when trials surface. It's probably one that was shared with you during your loss experience. I will admit there've been times when people shared this verse with me and I thought, *Yeah, yeah . . . I know. But I don't feel like He is really present at the moment.* Can you relate?

Let's examine this verse from a different angle and realize that we don't have to be in a state of trouble to go running to Him. God is there to help you, no matter what the situation—in seasons of blessing and in seasons of pain. Pregnancy after loss offers the best of both, literally.

Whether you are in a deep valley of grief, anxiety, and fear, or are rejoicing and confident with hope regarding this pregnancy, the promise that God is there to help you rings true in either extreme and amid everything in between. He is your refuge and strength, so press in close to Him either way. In doing so, He will be an ever-present help to you. And if we're honest, we all need a little help, right?

Dear God, help me to know the importance of seeking refuge in You. Strip me of any pride that stands in the way of coming to You and keep me humble. Wash away the fears and insecurities that keep me at a distance. Lord, You know my every need—physical, spiritual, emotional—and I pray that You would meet those needs in a tremendous way today and in the days ahead. In Jesus' name I pray. Amen.

pen the promise ———————————————————

What help do you need from God today?

Jesus Is with You

pregnancy promise

You can be sure that Jesus is with you forever.

"And surely I am with you always, to the very end of the age."

MATTHEW 28:20

Can you imagine being one of the women who discovered the empty tomb of Christ Jesus? What a miraculous turn of events! Throughout His earthly life, He had been clueing in the disciples that He would rise three days after death. It wasn't until He physically appeared back into their lives that they began to really understand. Thomas was especially doubtful when his fellow disciples told him that they had seen the risen Lord. In response, Thomas said, "Unless I see the nail marks in his hands and put my finger where the nails were, and put my hand into his side, I will not believe" (John 20:25). A week went by, they were all gathering again, and this time Thomas was there when Jesus joined them. Jesus approached Thomas and instructed, "Put your finger here; see my hands. Reach out your hand and put it into my side. Stop doubting and believe" (v. 27).

We are not unlike Thomas. Many times, seeing is believing. Our faith runs dry when we don't see what we hope for or desire. True faith means believing without the need to see. Jesus told Thomas during that exchange, "Because you have seen me, you have believed; blessed are those who have not seen and yet have believed" (v. 29).

In the gospel of Matthew, Jesus gives His disciples some important instructions as He prepares to depart from earth and ascend to heaven. He instructs them—us—to go and make disciples of all nations (Matt. 28:19). He assures us that He is with us to the very end of the age (v. 20). We are not left alone to navigate this world on our own. Jesus remained in Spirit with the disciples then, and He is with you now. If you have given your heart to Jesus, you can be sure that He is presently with you and that one day you will see Him face-to-face.

Dear heavenly Father, we cannot fathom Your power! You are mighty, indeed, to raise Jesus from the dead. Help me to have true faith, even when I cannot see. God, help me to know and feel the absolutely real and true presence of Christ in my life. Jesus, You tell us You are with us till the end of the age, and I believe You. Comfort me as I rest in the truth that You are with me now and forevermore. Amen.

pen the promise —————————

What is your reaction to the pregnancy promise above? Do you believe that Jesus is with you?

With You in the Fire

God is able to deliver me, and He will.

"If we are thrown into the blazing furnace, the God we serve is able to deliver us from it, and he will deliver us."

DANIEL 3:17

The story of Shadrach, Meshach, and Abednego found in the book of Daniel shows us an amazing level of faith. Threatened to be thrown into a blazing furnace if they did not bow down and worship a statue as King Nebuchadnezzar had instructed, these three brave men trusted in their God to deliver them from the blaze, and they stood firm in their faith. In our key verse, they declare that God is able to deliver them, and confidently proclaim that He will deliver them. What's more, these men tell the king, "But even if he does not, we want you to know, Your Majesty, that we will not serve your gods or worship the image of gold you have set up" (Dan. 3:18). God did, in fact, keep these men from being burned or harmed after being thrown into the fiery furnace, but their faith is demonstrated by their willingness to walk through the fire even if He hadn't delivered them.

Meri shared her version of such faith with me when she talked about her and her husband's struggle with infertility. They had to get to a place of trusting in God, relying on Jesus, even if they weren't able to conceive after having already experienced a miscarriage. Meri says, "I had to answer the question, Is Jesus enough? If the infertility treatments don't work, am I okay with being childfree?" These are hard questions to fathom and ones that some would say you can't know the answers to unless you are in that situation. For Meri, she had to resolve beforehand to believe Jesus was enough and trust that He was walking in the fire with her. The Jesus who kept Shadrach, Meshach, and Abednego safe in the furnace is the same Jesus Meri clung to in her own fire. He's the same Jesus you can cling to now. He is present. He is with you.

Dear God, You are mighty to save. You are able to deliver us from every fiery trial we face, yet sometimes You allow us to endure it—walking with us every step of the way—as you refine our faith in You. Lord, help me to know, believe, and sense Your very real presence in the fires that I face in my life. If it is Your will, I pray that You would deliver me from the fire of this trial, unscathed by the flames. In Jesus' name I pray. Amen.

pen the promise ────────────────────

Write your reaction to the faith of Shadrach, Meshach, and Abednego. Do you possess an "even if He does not" kind of faith?

The Promise of a Sovereign Refuge

peace in the promise ————————————

But as for me, it is good to be near God. I have made the Sovereign LORD my refuge; I will tell of all your deeds.

PSALM 73:28

As I think about God as our sovereign refuge, I ponder the wonderful sense of security that this promise brings. Throughout Scripture, we see His sovereign hand guiding and directing. Understanding that God is sovereign means realizing that He has complete power and authority over everything that happens. God is in control, even when it may seem as though life is spiraling out of control. Romans 8:28, which reads, "And we know that in all things God works for the good of those who love him, who have been called according to his purpose," is a great encouragement when it's hard for us to see what God is up to. Consider the nation of Israel. Their lives weren't easy and their journey was long and arduous, but the Sovereign Lord fulfilled His promise to them by bringing them out of captivity and into the Promised Land. Even in those most difficult of days, He was with them, protecting them and providing for them sometimes in ways unexpected. To be honest, they were sometimes ungrateful or discontent with His method of provision. It was their own sin and rebellion that kept them wandering in the wilderness for forty years. We are not unlike them.

Consider also our promised Messiah, Jesus, our Prince of Peace. Our heavenly Father's sovereign hand makes it possible for us to have a relationship with Him through His Son Jesus. Before the world began, God's plan of salvation would be our ultimate saving grace. This plan was made possible only by the sacrifice of His Son Jesus Christ on the cross. By His sacrifice, we are brought near and can seek safe refuge in Him. He's already welcomed our little ones into His kingdom and has made a way for us to be with Him, too. This gives us great reason to rejoice.

As we ponder the many ways that God's sovereignty is revealed through His Word, let us also consider how His sovereignty is currently at work in our lives. Circumstances can be hard, people can be hurtful, and emotions—though wonderful in so many ways—can be draining. When we look to our sovereign, faithful God we begin to see His plans unfold and take shape. This, my friends, is where we can take heart in knowing and believing that He has His best in store for us, even when the present may not seem to be good at all. After all, none of us would say that it was *good* that we've experienced loss. It downright stinks! In moments of pain as we remember our past, and in the present periods of uncertainty, fear, or worry, let us press in to the safe and secure refuge of our Sovereign Lord. As we draw near to Him, we can echo the words of the psalmist in our peace-in-the-promise verse above, "It is good to be near God" (Ps. 73:28).

Expecting with Hope

peace in the promise ―――――――――――――――

It is better to take refuge in the LORD than to trust in humans.

PSALM 118:8

We Aren't Going Anywhere, Baby

When my daughter, Aiyana, was four-and-a-half years old, her sense of security was shaken in a profound way. Our almost eighteen-year-old niece had lived with us since Aiyana was two years old. She was like a big sister to Aiyana. At Christmastime, our niece visited her grandmother on the other side of the family. Unbeknownst to us, she had secretly planned to not only visit her grandmother, but to stay and *live* with her grandmother. It was a time of deep hurt, chaos, and unresolved conflict in our family. As I write these words, one year since the time she left, tears well up at the thought of how the pain still runs deep—grief for the loss of the relationship and the tension that still exists. Most of all, I see the pain that her absence has caused in my daughter's tender heart. Even now, a year later, she worries about whether her daddy or I might not come home one day. Occasionally, she questions, "What if Daddy doesn't live with us anymore?" She's worried that we may leave, or die, or not be there to tuck her in or cook her supper. Her shaken sense of security, the plethora of questions, and the regressive behaviors are textbook grief in the life of a child her age.

The mommy within me rages over the innocence of her world being rocked by the reality that sometimes people do leave and cut ties. I can't count the number of times I've had to reassure Aiyana that she is safe, that I will always be there for her, and that no matter what, God is with her and she can trust Him and talk to Him about anything. As a mother with deep love and compassion for my daughter in this hurtful situation, I've done everything I can to console her and to reassure her of her safety and security. Many times, I've said: "We aren't going anywhere, baby. . . . We aren't going anywhere."

I think God wants to tell us the same thing. He's not going anywhere. Yet the promise of His sovereign refuge is far greater than the earthly promises any one of us can make as parents. He's absolutely not going anywhere. With utmost certainty, He will not change. We may run, hide, and flee from His presence. But the Lord remains faithful. We are safe in the refuge of His wings, under His care. Hebrews 13:8 declares, "Jesus Christ is the same yesterday and today and forever." James 1:17 reminds us, "Every good and perfect gift is from above, coming down from the Father of the heavenly lights, who does not change like shifting shadows." The gift of the child who grows within you comes from God, our Father, who *does not change.*

People change and promises are broken, but God is ever faithful. In Romans, Paul posed this question: "What if some were unfaithful? Will their unfaithfulness nullify God's faithfulness?" (3:3). In typical Paul fashion, he answered his own question with a strong response: "Not at all! Let God be true, and every human being a liar" (v. 4). It may seem harsh, but it's the sad truth. Only the Lord knows, but I can't imagine any human being who hasn't lied, other than Jesus, of course. That's the difference between God and man. God is faithful in all that He is and all that He does. Try as we might, we fail miserably. I've failed miserably. I'm willing to guess that you can think of a time (or two) when you've failed, as well. Humans are naturally sinful. God is naturally holy. Thus, His disposition toward us is love, mercy, and faithfulness.

peace in the promise ————————————————

For the word of the LORD is right and true; he is faithful in all he does.

PSALM 33:4

Surveying the Psalms

Truly, all of God's Word is evidence of His sovereignty. The Psalms, in particular, speak clearly of God as our Sovereign refuge,

Expecting with Hope

showing us the secure embrace He has over our lives and the lives of our babies. A simple word study reveals that the word *sovereign* appears in Scripture more than three hundred times and *refuge* appears in Scripture upwards of one hundred times, depending on the translation. The book of Ezekiel has the most references to the "Sovereign Lord." God Himself repeats this classic message throughout this book of the Bible nearly sixty times: "Then they [you] will know that I am the Sovereign Lord."

The Psalms include seven references to our "Sovereign Lord." As I poured over these particular verses, I was struck by how the words give us an amazing depiction of God's character:

He's a God who saves (Ps. 68:20).
He's our hope (Ps. 71:5).
He performs mighty deeds (Pss. 71:16; 73:28).
He's our refuge (Pss. 73:28; 141:8).
He's our help, because of His good love (Ps. 109:21).
He's our deliverer (Ps. 140:7).
He's our shield (Ps. 140:7).

We could go on and on studying each of these traits and find verse after verse to support every single one of these attributes of our Sovereign Lord. As you reflect upon your past and examine your current situation, mull over this list and ponder how God has shown Himself strong in these areas of your life. How has He been your hope? Your deliverer? Your refuge and your shield? When we are able to see the faithfulness of God in our past, it can be easier for us to trust in His faithfulness toward us in our present. Take inventory; how is the Sovereign Lord showing His faithfulness to you today?

There may be fear and anxiety and a whole mix of emotions from the past that are overshadowing the true joy of this pregnancy. Peel back the layers, sweet friend, and take a closer look at your present situation and marvel at the miracle of it all. You are pregnant with a child;

a precious baby who the Lord continues to knit together in *your* womb. You have been chosen to be this baby's mother. Only the Lord knows without a doubt how much time you will be blessed with this child, but instead of worrying over what *could* happen, why not relish in what you know to be true today? Just as the Sovereign Lord promises to be your refuge through it all, He, too, is the refuge for your baby.

As I continued with my word study, I discovered more than forty references to our God as a "refuge" within the Psalms. Reading over these verses, I saw the amazing benefits of seeking refuge in the Sovereign Lord. According to these verses, the one who seeks refuge in God is:

safe (Pss. 16:1; 37:40)
shielded (Pss. 18:30; 91:4; 119:114; 144:2)
rescued (Pss. 17:7; 18:2; 25:20; 31:2; 34:22; 71:3)
glad (Ps. 5:11)
blessed (Pss. 2:12; 31:19; 34:8)
rejoicing (Pss. 5:11; 64:10)
delivered (Pss. 18:2; 31:1; 37:40; 144:2)
fulfilled (Ps. 142:5)
giving God glory (Ps. 64:10)

How would you say your current state of heart and mind lines up with the list of characteristics above? Can you say with certainty that you are safe, shielded, and glad? Are you rejoicing, and do you consider yourself blessed? Are you fulfilled? Are you glorifying God with your attitude and life? If I'm honest, I take a look at this list and tinges of envy come to the surface because I desperately want to experience the characteristics portrayed by the psalmist. I guess it's time to seek refuge in the Sovereign Lord.

Too often, we allow our circumstances and our feelings about said circumstances to dictate the attitude of our hearts, and ultimately, our joy. This may come as a surprise to you, but joy is not a feeling. Rather, joy is a reflection of who we are in Him. As we allow the Sovereign Lord to be our refuge, as He draws us close and keeps us safe under the shadow of His wings, we have great reason to rejoice. We have a God who lavishes His love upon us and who protects us in ways we can't begin to understand. Sometimes, such love and protection may appear to be nothing more than absence, silence, or heartbreaking loss. In all actuality, every painstaking experience and every unanswered prayer are merely tiny pieces of a grander puzzle that He is piecing together in accord with His loving, merciful, sovereign plan for our lives. The mighty God of the Bible who parted seas, filled the barren womb, and brought the dead to life is the same God who dotes over you and the precious babe that you carry now. Yes, He loves you. He is your sovereign refuge and there is great hope in Him.

peace in the promise ———————————————

"Blessed is she who has believed that the Lord would fulfill his promises to her!"

LUKE 1:45

Hannah, Ruth, Mary . . . Sally, Susie, Sherry

There is much to learn about the Lord, our sovereign refuge, and His ever-present and loving involvement in every aspect of our lives. In this section, we will take a glimpse into the lives of three women of the Bible—Hannah, Ruth, and Mary—and see how God's sovereignty was evident in their lives. We must bear in mind that some of God's promises are specific to individuals, while others are promises for all humanity. For example, Mary was chosen to bear the Son of God in her womb. The promise of her pregnancy was God's plan to bring the Messiah into the world. Mary embraced the promise to bear the Son of God, Jesus, who was conceived by the Holy Spirit. Pregnancy, childbirth, and motherhood are not guaranteed for everyone. There are, however, promises for all humanity to claim. Jesus was born into this world so that all of mankind could have fellowship with the Father by believing in Jesus, our promised Prince of Peace. John 3:16 makes this promise for all humanity by declaring, "For God so loved the world that he gave his one and only son, that whoever believes in him shall not perish but have eternal life." In all things, we can rest in the assurance of God's loving refuge, His faithfulness, and His sovereign hand in our circumstances. You don't have to be a hero of the faith, part of the lineage of Jesus, or some superstar Christian (as if there were such a thing) to identify God's loving, sovereign work in your life.

Hannah

We find Hannah's story at the beginning of 1 Samuel, rightfully so, as Samuel was the son she bore after years of waiting, longing, and pleading for a child. Thankfully, in today's culture, none of us would likely find ourselves in the marital scenario that Hannah did; she was one of two wives to her husband, Elkanah. His other wife, Peninnah, bore many children to him, but "the LORD had closed Hannah's womb" (1 Sam. 1:6). Peninnah continually provoked and irritated Hannah, flaunting her children in front of her, while Hannah remained childless. First Samuel 1:7 says, "This went on year after year. Whenever Hannah went up to the house of the LORD, her rival provoked her till she wept and would not eat." I can't imagine how difficult that must have been. It's difficult enough to face pregnant relatives, friends, and even strangers when longing for a child or grieving the loss of a child.

In her lament, Hannah cried out to the Lord in prayer asking for a son, yet surrendering him to the Lord's service should her longing for a child be fulfilled. The Lord did, in fact, bless Hannah with a child whom she named Samuel. When he was weaned from nursing, she took him to the temple and explained to the priest Eli that this was the child she had prayed for and whom she had committed to the Lord. In 1 Samuel 1:27–28, Hannah explains, "I prayed for this child, and the

LORD has granted me what I asked of him. So now I give him to the LORD. For his whole life he will be given over to the LORD."

As I consider Hannah's story, I am struck by her faith and her obedience. After all, I can think of many times where I've prayed and pleaded and outright bargained with God. Most, if not all, of my pleas have been selfish in nature, whereas Hannah exhibits a great selflessness. She meant what she said when she surrendered her child-to-be over to the Lord and was given the opportunity to make her faith known by actually physically relinquishing Samuel to Eli's care after he was weaned.

I wonder: would Hannah have been so willing to commit Samuel to the Lord had she not had to endure years of waiting for this blessing? While we don't get a record of Hannah's innermost thoughts and feelings during this period of her life, we do know these facts: she had a deep longing for children, but was barren (1 Sam. 1:1–9); Peninnah continually provoked and irritated her (v. 6); and she experienced "great anguish and grief" (v. 16). As I reflect upon what we know about Hannah and the birth of her son, Samuel, it appears as though the Lord used that period of waiting, longing, grief, and anguish in Hannah's life in some tremendous ways. He brought her to a point of absolute surrender and total obedience, and we see His wonderful redemption at work in and through her heart and circumstances.

Ask yourself: How has the Lord used my waiting, longing, grief, and anguish to refine me? Have I let Him? If not, what areas do I need to surrender in order for Him to work through me now?

Ruth

Ruth was no stranger to grief. Widowed as a young wife, it was her very circumstances that brought her to faith in the one true God, our Sovereign Lord. I encourage you to read the book of Ruth for yourself, but for our purposes here, I will provide a short recap. It starts with a woman named Naomi, her husband, and their two sons, Mahlon and Kilion. Due to famine in the land, Naomi and her family fled from

Bethlehem to Moab, seeking relief. Naomi's husband died, and then her two sons each married Moabite women, Ruth becoming the wife of Mahlon. Within ten years of her husband's death, Naomi's sons died as well. As you might imagine, Naomi was in deep anguish over these tremendous losses. Upon her return to her homeland, Naomi addressed the people by saying, "'Don't call me Naomi,' she told them. 'Call me Mara, because the Almighty has made my life very bitter'" (Ruth 1:20). Ruth, wife of Mahlon, was in great distress, too, yet she remained faithful to Naomi, even after her husband's death, despite these instructions from her mother-in-law:

> "Go back, each of you, to your mother's home. May the LORD show you kindness, as you have shown kindness to your dead husbands and to me. May the LORD grant that each of you will find rest in the home of another husband." (Ruth 1:8–9)

Naomi's other daughter-in-law, Orpah, obeyed Naomi and returned to her home and her gods, while Ruth insisted on accompanying Naomi back to her homeland of Bethlehem. Despite Naomi's insistence that Ruth return to her own homeland and her gods (because Moabites did not worship the God of Israel), Ruth replied:

> "Don't urge me to leave you or to turn back from you. Where you go I will go, and where you stay I will stay. Your people will be my people and your God my God. Where you die I will die, and there I will be buried. May the LORD deal with me, be it ever so severely, if even death separates you and me." (Ruth 1:16–17)

Consequently, Ruth accompanied Naomi back to Bethlehem, and it was there where she met Boaz. As a cousin of Ruth's deceased husband, Boaz had the right and responsibility to take care of his relative's mother and wife, Naomi and Ruth. Through a series of circumstances,

Boaz and Ruth became acquainted with one another, and he willingly took Ruth to be his wife. They gave birth to a son, Obed, who would become the grandfather of King David, a forefather of Jesus.

Sometimes it's the most difficult journey we travel that brings us to faith in God. For Ruth, the journey included the grief of being widowed, and leaving her homeland, family, and faith to follow the path of a self-proclaimed bitter mother-in-law who served the one true God. In doing so, Ruth was welcomed into the family of God by faith; married to Boaz, her kinsman redeemer; and became part of the lineage of Jesus Himself.

As we ponder this powerful story of redemption, let's take a look inward. Like Ruth, we are no strangers to grief. Have we allowed our journey to bring us to faith and commitment to the Sovereign Lord? Are we able to look back and see His guiding hand and faithfulness along the way? Perhaps you've never thought of it. Take a step back, try to capture an aerial view of your journey, and ask God to reveal a glimpse of His redemption to you now.

Mary

We are all familiar with the story of Mary and the amazing promise that God fulfilled in her life, choosing her to bear His one and only Son Jesus. Our peace-in-the-promise verse from Luke 1:45 speaks directly of Mary: "Blessed is she who has believed that the Lord would fulfill his promises to her!"

In our case, the promise is not the guarantee of a healthy baby born alive and well, and the promise may not be affirmed by the audible voice or visit from an angel. Rather, the promise is the truth that God is our sovereign refuge always, healthy child or not. This, my friends, is where we must forge a stake in the ground and claim our joy. Our joy is in Him alone as we stand firm in His promises. He is our sovereign refuge. He has a good and perfect plan in store for each and every one of us. He is love. His love drives out fear, and we love only because He first loved us. He is real and present and with us now on in to tomorrow. These promises and more give us reason to rejoice, regardless of the trials that this life brings.

These precious women's stories are relevant for us to consider in light of our own stories that matter to God, the author of them all. There is heartbreak along their paths, but not without the absolute beauty of redemption that can only come from our Sovereign Lord, whose perfect plan prevails. Even when it's hard, it's for His glory and our good, and we can always run to Him, our sovereign refuge.

My Pregnancy Prayer for You

Sovereign Lord, You are a strong and mighty refuge. We can trust in You to keep us safe and secure. We have seen Your faithfulness and trust in You to be ever faithful according to Your steadfast love. Lord, please be with this woman now, as she wrestles with the pain of her past and the joy of her present. Be her refuge, Lord, when times are hard and when anxiety weighs her down. Help her to trust in You as she continues to carry this baby, each day a day closer to meeting her precious little one. Help her to remember that You are sovereign and Your plans are good. We pray these things in the name of Jesus. Amen.

Refuge in His Wings

pregnancy promise ─────────────────────────

There is refuge for you in God.

He will cover you with his feathers, and under his wings you will find refuge; his faithfulness will be your shield and rampart.

PSALM 91:4

Jessica learned through her loss and pregnancy experiences to rely on God's sovereignty. She experienced two pregnancy losses in 2010, and subsequently became pregnant with twins. She had hoped and prayed for twins, and God heard and answered her prayer, as she gave birth to twin boys. They were diagnosed in utero with twin-to-twin transfusion syndrome (TTTS), but were born alive, thrived, and are growing strong today.

Jessica shares what God taught her during this time of high-risk pregnancy after loss. Amid the confusion, worry, and hope, she says, "I had to rely on the fact that I knew He had a plan. That He was in control. But I had a hard time believing that He was good." It's one thing to *know* He is good and that He has a plan. It's an entirely different thing to believe it. Sometimes our hearts need time to catch up to our minds. Jessica had already experienced the loss of two babies and was now pregnant with twin boys who, quite possibly, would join their siblings in heaven. As she reflects on her past experience with loss and the early health challenges of her twins who are thriving today, Jessica acknowledges God's goodness when she says, "With the circumstances around the babies [pleading to God for twins] and their health issues, I knew that He was good . . . He was my refuge in a quiet way."

Jessica's relationship with God during her pregnancy with the twins was intimate and personal and proved to be a time when she found rest in Him. You may find that sometimes others think they know what's best for you. Jessica shares her encounter with one such woman:

> There was one woman in particular who was really pushy with me regarding my faith at the time [during the pregnancy with the twins]. She thought I should spend all my time on bed rest studying God's Word and doing [Bible] studies. But that's not the kind of intimacy that I had with God. We had a strong relationship that was real, honest, and authentic. I prayed a lot, but it was more like a daily conversation than a time set aside for prayer. I cried, praised, clung, wept, and poured out my fear and need for control.

Jessica shared openly and honestly what it was that got her through those difficult days of pregnancy after loss, and it wasn't following someone else's idea of what her relationship with God should look like. It was seeking Him more, in her own way, through prayer and surrender. She pressed in under the refuge of His wings, and He was faithful to meet her there with a blanket of protection. He will do the same for you too, friend.

Dear God, You are a mighty, sovereign refuge. Under Your wings, there is safety, security, and refuge. Help me, Lord, to seek You in a real and personal way like Jessica did. Lead me, Lord, as I grow in my relationship with You. I want to know You more, God. Help me to trust in Your sovereign plan for my life and for the life of the baby whom You've blessed me with now. Amen.

pen the promise ————————————————

What is your reaction to Jessica's story of viewing God as her sovereign refuge? Write about it in your journal.

Expecting with Hope

Hiding Place

pregnancy promise ——————————————————————

Let God be your hiding place.

You are my hiding place; you will protect me from trouble and surround me with songs of deliverance.

PSALM 32:7

As children, we all had our favorite hideout. Mine was in the "secret stairway" that led from my parents' closet down to the kitchen in our old two-story house. I'd run there just to be alone or when I felt alone. As an adult, I confess that I still hide out at times. I no longer have a secret staircase, but I do have a favorite sitting chair in my bedroom. It's placed by a window that peers out the front of the second story of our cozy bungalow. I no longer flee to my hiding place to be alone. Rather, I go there to be with God.

Sometimes I start my day there, and other times I end my day there. Some days, I hide away in the comforts of my sitting chair with tears leaking and my mouth whispering, "Jesus come," as troubles threaten to consume. Soon enough, the peace of God—my true and only hiding place—surrounds me, and I get lost in Him.

When troubles rise, worries well up, and you just want to run and hide, run directly into the open and loving arms of God. If you don't have a "hiding place" of your own, where you can go to be still before the Lord, create a space today. Make a point to spend time there with Him. He longs to be your hiding place.

Sovereign Lord, You are my hiding place. You protect me, You deliver me, and You provide me with a sense of security, even when the world around me seems so unsure. Lord, be with me now and give me the strength to run to You for refuge. Keep me safe and secure and be my hiding place, oh God. When troubles come, when doubts set in, when the days are long and hard, help me to seek and find refuge in You alone. Amen.

pen the promise —————————————————

In your journal, write down your "hiding place." If you do not have one, create a space in your home where you can spend time alone with God. Write about a time during this pregnancy when you found refuge with God.

Shield Me, Lord

pregnancy promise ————————————————————

The Lord is my shield.

As for God, his way is perfect: The LORD's word is flawless; he shields all who take refuge in him.

PSALM 18:30

Kim sensed God's protection during pregnancy with her little girl, Anna. Like me, and perhaps like you, Kim was afraid of the possibility of another loss, having already lost her daughter, Gabrielle, to anencephaly. While Anna was born alive, several complications became apparent after her birth. Kim recalled, "My fears increased after I found out that Anna had a heart condition." She went on to share how God had been a shield to her during pregnancy, by saying, "God spared me from finding out until after she was born, though. I had a fetal echocardiogram which should have shown her problem at twenty-six weeks, but it didn't."

As for little Anna, Kim reported, "God has protected Anna's little heart so far. She has never had any major symptoms after her first few months of her condition. It may be years before she needs her heart valve replaced. Normally a child with her condition needs surgery before three years old. She is nearly nine years old now."

The Lord's shield of protection is so evident in Kim's story and can be an encouragement to each one of us. Whatever you're going through now, the Lord knows. He is with you, shielding and protecting you every step of the way. Take refuge in Him as you await your child's arrival and ask Him in prayer to shield you from whatever may come your way.

Dear God, You are our refuge and our shield. I praise You for Your mighty hand of protection in Kim and Anna's lives, and I pray that same blanket of protection will be extended over me and my precious child. I know, Lord, that every journey will look different; no two paths are the same. But You are the same unchanging, faithful God for those who take refuge in You. Amen.

pen the promise ———————————————————

Write the ways that you have sensed the Lord's protection over you during this pregnancy.

He Is My Rock

pregnancy promise ————————————————————

God is my fortress!

Truly he is my rock and my salvation; he is my fortress, I will not be shaken.

PSALM 62:6

Just this past year, I saw the mountains for the very first time. Till then, the only glimpse I'd had of them was the aerial view from a plane heading elsewhere. Pikes Peak sure does provide an amazing change of scenery from the flat, rolling cornfields of Iowa. When I caught my first sight of the mountains, my eyes welled up with tears. My husband thought I was crazy, but I was just overcome with emotion as I took in the majesty of God's magnificent creation. As a part of our stay in Colorado, we had the opportunity to explore a bit, and I can't recall the number of times that I just sat back and said, "Wow!"

Everything about the mountains was simply breathtaking. When I considered that God made these mountains by simply breathing them into existence, I was blown away. As strong and mighty as the mountains may have seemed to me, I look at God and I realize He is stronger. He is a mighty fortress. He is the rock of my salvation when the world seems to be crumbling apart. He is steadfast and never changing, even when my circumstances change.

LeeAnn shared a similar sentiment when she thought back to her experiences of loss and pregnancy after loss, and described God in this way: "God was my hope, my rock, [and] my peace of mind when I started to doubt. I knew God had been there for me during my loss, and He was there for me during my pregnancy after loss." Can you relate to her words? May God be your rock, your refuge, your hope, and your mighty fortress during this time.

Mighty God, You are all-powerful. You are my rock and my refuge, my mighty fortress. Though at times life has crumbled around me, You have been there to keep me safe. Even now as I struggle with fear and worries, I can trust in You to be my rock and keep me safe. Help me, God, to trust in You. When my heart and mind wander, lovingly bring me back into Your safe embrace. In Jesus' name I pray. Amen.

pen the promise

Do you view God as your rock and fortress? Who or what do you tend to run to during difficult times?

Daily Burdens

pregnancy promise —————————————————————————

The Sovereign Lord saves us and bears our burdens daily.

"Praise be to the Lord, to God our Savior, who daily bears our burdens. Our God is a God who saves; from the Sovereign LORD comes escape from death."

PSALM 68:19–20

Just as this key verse says, God *daily* bears our burdens. He's the God who cares to be intimately involved with the daily aspects of our lives. It's in how we handle the day-to-day that we are able to most authentically and genuinely reflect who we are in Him.

In the situation of pregnancy after loss, others look on with great optimism and view the experience as something that will be over in just a few months. But for the woman who's expecting, just getting through the day can be a challenge. This is especially true when that nine-month time span will most likely overlap with some significant days that remind you of your child who died. It could be a due date, an anniversary date, or a special holiday—Mother's Day for example. On those days, especially, it's hard to know whether to mourn or to celebrate.

Every day will be different; some more challenging than others. The important thing is to be sure to include Jesus in your daily walk on this journey. He is with you, is for you, and desires to bear your burdens each day. No crisis is too complicated for Him, no emotion too complex, and no simple pleasure too light for Him to care about. He is a God of details and cares about every single one.

Heavenly Father, thank You for being the God who saves me from sin and death. Thank You for Your merciful love that welcomed my child into Your presence, and thank You for Your love that You extend to me and my baby who grows within. You are good, Lord, and I know that You desire to bear my burdens each and every day. Help me to trust You with my cares. Help me to remember that nothing is too hard for You and that You care even about the simplest things and want to rejoice with me. Amen.

pen the promise ————————————————

How can you allow Jesus to bear your burdens daily? Write your ideas in your journal.

The Promise of Provision

peace in the promise ————————————————

And to provide for those who grieve in Zion—to bestow on them a crown of beauty instead of ashes, the oil of joy instead of mourning, and a garment of praise instead of a spirit of despair.

ISAIAH 61:3

At the beginning of Jesus' public ministry, He is found in the temple reading from the prophet Isaiah:

> "The Spirit of the Lord is on me, because he has anointed me to proclaim good news to the poor. He has sent me to proclaim freedom for the prisoners and recovery of sight for the blind, to set the oppressed free, to proclaim the year of the Lord's favor." (Luke 4:18–19, quoting Isa. 61:1–2)

After reading from the scroll, He sat down and said, "Today this scripture is fulfilled in your hearing" (Luke 4:21), revealing Himself as the promised Messiah. Jesus was and is the good news. The prophet Isaiah foretold Jesus' coming and said that He would be the one who sets us free: free from oppression, free from grief, free from despair. Jesus has the power to set us free from the things of this world that keep us in bondage.

For those of us who've had the experience of pregnancy after loss, we know well the need for the Lord's provision. Sometimes the needs are material, but most often the needs are emotional and spiritual as we wrestle with the contrasting emotions of grief and joy. Isaiah foretold the promise that our Messiah would come and He would bestow upon grievers "a crown of beauty instead of ashes, the oil of joy instead of mourning, and a garment of praise instead of a spirit of despair" (Isa. 61:3).

As I've ministered to many women over the years, it is not uncommon for me to hear that some women, in the aftermath of loss, believe that the *only* thing that will bring them joy again is to become pregnant and give birth to another child. Perhaps you can relate. Or maybe you are like me and vowed you'd never become pregnant again in the aftermath of loss. In either case, we are grossly misled, because the source of our joy (another child or no more children) is misplaced. True, lasting joy comes from Jesus. *He* will bestow upon us the oil of joy and a crown of beauty in place of mourning and ashes, but it's up to Him to determine exactly what this will look like. Sometimes, we don't see how He's provided until some time passes and we are able to look back in retrospect. Other times, we see Him at work in the midst of our circumstances, providing in ways that are only possibly by God.

Jehovah Jireh, God Our Provider

There are many names for God found in Scripture. *Jehovah Jireh* means "God Our Provider" and is found only once in the Bible. That being said, its use in the story of Abraham and his son Isaac is an amazing example of the Lord's provision. Abraham and his wife, Sarah, had to wait well into old age before being blessed with a son, whom the Lord God had promised. God had promised Abraham that his offspring would be as numerous as the stars. Abraham believed the Lord's promise, and his faith was credited to him as righteousness (Gen. 15:6). But Sarah took matters into her own hands. She offered her maidservant, Hagar, to be Abraham's wife so that they might bear a son. Hagar, indeed, became pregnant, but Sarah began to despise her and the child she bore. Hagar fled from Sarah's mistreatment but eventually returned when an angel of the Lord appeared and instructed her to do so. In Genesis 21, we learn that the Lord ultimately fulfilled His promise to Abraham and Sarah through the birth of their son Isaac, despite the attempt that they made to "help God out" by involving Hagar, who birthed Ishmael.

Some time after the birth of Isaac, God put Abraham to the ultimate test. In Genesis 22:2, the Lord instructed him, "Take your son, your only son, whom you love—Isaac—and go to the region of Moriah. Sacrifice him there as a burnt offering on a mountain I will show you."

While we don't know the precise age of Isaac at this time, this account in Genesis tells us that he was big and strong enough to carry wood for the burnt offering. I can't imagine what was going through Abraham's heart and mind in response to the Lord's command. When you read the account in Scripture, you see that Abraham obeyed immediately. He did not argue, bargain, or plead with God for some sort of escape clause. He simply packed up and left, along with Isaac and two servants, to do as the Lord had commanded.

When they reached the mountain, Abraham said to his servants, "Stay here with the donkey while I and the boy go over there. We will worship and then we will come back to you" Gen. 22:5). He had faith that they would *both* return to the servants. As they proceeded up the mountain, Isaac said to his father, "The fire and wood are here, . . . but where is the lamb for the burnt offering?" (v. 7). Abraham confidently told Isaac, "God himself will provide the lamb for the burnt offering, my son" (v. 8). As surely as Abraham had believed, God did provide. Just as Abraham reached for his knife to sacrifice Isaac, God called out from heaven and said, "Do not lay a hand on the boy. . . . Do not do anything to him. Now I know that you fear God, because you have not withheld from me your son, your only son" (Gen. 22:12). When Abraham looked up, there was a ram available for him to sacrifice, and so he did.

peace in the promise ──────────────

So Abraham called that place The LORD Will Provide. And to this day it is said, "On the mountain of the LORD it will be provided."

GENESIS 22:14

In the biblical account of Abraham and Isaac, the Lord provided the offering to use in Isaac's place. God intervened and stopped Abraham from truly sacrificing Isaac. Abraham's faith was proved genuine as he was ready to do as the Lord had asked, as difficult and absolutely unimaginable as it may have seemed. This Old Testament story is a picture of what Jesus did for each of us. He came down to earth, lived a perfect life, and died upon the cross *in our place.* God the Father knew that we would need a Savior, and He intervened by providing His only Son. Such provision meets our greatest need in life: to be rescued from our sin with eternity secured in heaven.

But as we live our everyday lives, we encounter numerous needs: material, physical, emotional, and spiritual. If we were to list our needs on paper, chances are we would be able to take a second look and see that many of our so-called needs are nothing more than worldly desires. We truly have very few needs in life. With that perspective, it becomes much easier to see just how truly blessed we are. God knows what we need better than we do, and He is faithful to provide.

Patricia shared her story of entrusting God with her and her unborn child's needs when she was pregnant after the loss of three babies. In 2011, she lost her son during pregnancy at eighteen weeks along. The following year, she experienced the loss of twins at twelve weeks along. She struggled to accept the fact that despite financial struggles and ultrasounds that revealed concerns during her third and most recent pregnancy, God was in control. She was unable to afford further testing and medications and literally had to put it all in God's hands. She explained:

> I had to trust that my lack of financial ability, and the less-than-reassuring ultrasound scans were not too big for God to handle. I had to place my faith in the fact that God's plan for my baby did not depend on my money and did not depend on anything other than God's will and greater plan. I had to place my faith in the ideas that God did not face financial constraints or medical constraints and that His sovereign power was not limited by circumstance. After sleepless nights, anxiety, grief, and tears, I found my faith grow.

In February of 2013, Patricia delivered a healthy baby girl. Her testimony is truly one of trusting in God's provision. Not only did He provide provision for her physical and material needs, but through it all, she found her faith grow in Him.

Whittled Down, Like Gideon

In chapters six and seven of the Old Testament book of Judges we meet Gideon. Gideon was appointed by the Lord to lead the Israelites in battle to defeat the Midianites. As Gideon rallied the troops, so to speak . . . "The LORD said to Gideon, 'You have too many men. I cannot deliver Midian into their hands, or Israel would boast against me, "My own strength has saved me"'" (Judg. 7:2). Gideon was commanded to tell the army that anyone who was afraid could leave. As a result, twenty-two thousand men left, leaving ten thousand to fight the battle. Still, the Lord told Gideon that there were too many men. So Gideon did as the Lord instructed and took them down to the water where the men were told to drink. They were separated based on how they drank the water: those who lapped the water with their tongues, as opposed to cupping the water in their hands, were commanded to stay and fight the battle. By this method, Gideon's army was whittled down to three hundred men. The army started out with more than thirty-two thousand and now held just a fraction of that number. The Lord saw fit to do this so that He could receive all the honor and glory for the mighty victory that would soon be won, and so that evidence of God's provision would be apparent to all who saw the events. As the Lord had promised, the Midianites were delivered into the hands of Gideon and his army, and victory rested with the Lord.

There is much to learn from the battle against the Midianites. God decreased the size of Gideon's army so that He would be praised and His provision would be recognized. Perhaps, the Lord allows us to be whittled down—like Gideon—so that when others look on, they can see that our deliverance, the redemption, or the battle won was possible only due to the divine work and intervention of our mighty God.

Through it all, we don't have to be afraid. God knows our needs and is in complete control. Judges 6:23–24 reads:

> But the LORD said to him, "Peace! Do not be afraid. You are not going to die."
> So Gideon built an altar to the LORD there and called it The LORD is Peace. To this day it stands in Ophrah of the Abiezrites.

The Lord is peace! Jesus is the Prince of Peace. When we trust in our sovereign, almighty, in-control God who provides, there is great peace; peace that passes all understanding. Still, we must take our burdens to the Lord. Paul gave us wise instruction when he wrote, "Do not be anxious about anything, but in every situation, by prayer and petition, with thanksgiving, present your requests to God. And the peace of God, which transcends all understanding, will guard your hearts and your minds in Christ Jesus" (Phil. 4:6–7). In other words, be thankful, be prayerful, and pour your heart out to God. He protects, and He brings peace.

 *peace in the promise* —————————————————

"Therefore do not worry about tomorrow, for tomorrow will worry about itself. Each day has enough trouble of its own."

MATTHEW 6:34

Don't Worry

Telling a woman who's pregnant after the experience of miscarriage or infant loss, "Don't worry," is like telling a really grumpy coworker on Monday morning to "cheer up." The requested outcome is not likely to happen; the woman who is pregnant after loss won't stop worrying, and the cranky coworker won't be more cheerful at your command. Your suggestions may actually have the opposite effect.

I struggle with control (in case I hadn't been clear about that by now). When things aren't going according to plan, or if there's too much noise, or if I'm feeling really crowded in a busy department store, etc., I get irritable and clench up. I have to stand still, refocus, and work hard to change my attitude and perspective. In these tight moments, my husband has been known to say this well-intentioned phrase, often with a gentle and loving tone: "Calm down, Tesk . . ." Aaagggh! I'm not going to calm down, especially when *you* tell me to. He's learned the hard way not to say that to me. I should also say I've learned not to lash out if and when he does say it. In my estimation, telling the woman who is pregnant after loss, "Don't worry," ranks right up there with the "You're so strong" *compliment* that we all love (hate).

As much as we may not want to hear it, these are precisely the words of Jesus. Matthew 6:25 records Jesus stating plainly, "Therefore I tell you, do not worry about your life." He then lists two of our most basic needs: food and clothing. Our peace-in-the-promise verse above encourages us to focus on the here and now. In it, Jesus tells us that we shouldn't worry about tomorrow because tomorrow will have its own troubles and we can deal with them when that day comes. I don't know about you, but I am not so bold as to verbally yell back at Jesus. At the same time, I know that my actions—whether or not I've said a word—too often reflect disobedience, especially in this particular area. It seems impossible to simply stop doing something that comes so naturally, at least for a chronic worrier like me. Then I am reminded that this too can be overcome because of the new life I have in Christ. Ephesians 4:22–24 encourages us:

> You were taught, with regard to your former way of life, to put off your old self, which is being corrupted by its deceitful desires; to be made new in the attitude of your minds; and to put on the new self, created to be like God in true righteousness and holiness.

If we've surrendered our hearts to Jesus, the Holy Spirit indwells our hearts, giving us power to live our lives in full obedience to God's instructions. God knows that we need more help than the simple command, "Do not worry."

So Jesus gives us clear instruction as to what we *should* do in Matthew 6:33: "But seek first his kingdom and his righteousness, and all these things will be given to you as well." Jesus is not telling us that if we seek His kingdom He will give us what we want. Rather, He is instructing us not to be so wrapped up and consumed by the worries of this world that we fail to put Him first. He's calling us to seek Him first in all things and reminding us that He knows our *needs*, for which He is sure to provide.

My Pregnancy Prayer for You

Dear Lord, You are in control! You know our needs better than we do, and You are continually faithful to take care of us. Lord, I pray that You would show the wonders of Your provision to the woman who reads here now. I pray that You would bestow upon her a sense of Your great peace as You provide. I pray that You would bless in ways unexpected—both materially and spiritually. Help this dear mom to trust in You with everything. Amen.

Seek First

pregnancy promise ————————————————————

Seek God's kingdom first.
"But seek first his kingdom and his righteousness, and all these things will be given to you as well."

MATTHEW 6:33

What is the first thing you think about when you wake up each morning? Does your mind race with thoughts or concerns about the baby? Do you reach for your smart phone to check emails, messages, or social media? Do you run through that internal to-do list and wonder how it's all going to get done? Do you think on things that are lovely, admirable, praiseworthy—things of the Lord?

I pose these questions because I think the answers to them are a good indicator of what beckons our immediate attention. For me, I usually awaken and instantly think about getting up and helping my family get going. Most days, I try to get up at least fifteen minutes before I know the rest of the family will be up so that I can brew a hot cup of coffee and sit down with the Lord. It doesn't always happen.

What might our days look like if we sought out God first as we rise each morning, as well as in various decisions and circumstances? I can tell you honestly that the days I start with Jesus are the days that are, overall, more peaceful. Not because of circumstances, other people's attitudes, or the schedule of events. Rather, it's the attitude of my heart and the intentional focus I made that day to seek Him first. I want to be better at seeking Him first. Won't you join me?

Dear God, I want to seek You and Your kingdom first, above all things. Help me, Lord, to do that. Give me peace about my day and about my circumstances as I seek to know You more, do Your will, and follow hard after You. Lord, I know that You care about every aspect of my life and You will provide for all my needs. In Your name I pray. Amen.

pen the promise ——————————————————

Seek God now. How is He working in your current situation and showing you His hand of provision? Write about it in your journal.

I'm Not a Failure

pregnancy promise ————————————————————

God is my strength.

"My flesh and my heart may fail, but God is the strength of my heart and my portion forever."

PSALM 73:26

Have you ever felt like a failure in your journey to motherhood? I certainly have. When we experienced our first loss, we were told that the chromosomal abnormality and accompanying brain condition that she was diagnosed with was a fluke occurrence. Nothing that we did or could have done differently would've prevented it. A random mix-up of the genes, the doctor said. I hated that it happened, but eventually came to a place of peace as time went by and the Lord drew me near.

We went on to have a healthy girl after Chloe, but then experienced two more miscarriages. I vividly recall the emotions that roiled to the surface. I had failed again. I'd failed my husband. I'd failed my family. My own body had failed my children. I figured I was nothing more than a failure as a mother . . . and as a woman. Sigh.

I know now, with great certainty and confidence, that I am not a failure. And neither are you. Yes, we may *feel* like failures, but we are not. Our hearts fail. Our flesh fails. Both are a result of sin in this fallen, failing world. But the encouragement from Scripture is this: God is the strength of our hearts and our portion forever. He is our portion. He is our strength.

When you feel as though you are failing, doubt whether the Lord will sustain the baby who now grows within, or are paralyzed by the fear of yet another loss, remember this: God is the strength of your heart. He is for you, no matter what the outcome may be.

Dear God, help me to journey through this pregnancy with confidence, regardless of my past. I admit, Lord, that I have felt like a failure at times. I rebuke that lie now and ask that You would help me to look forward with eyes fixed on You. Bring things to mind that remind me that You are all I need, You are my portion, and You are my strength. Amen.

pen the promise —————————————————————

Have you ever felt like a failure in your journey to motherhood? What is the truth of the matter?

Expecting with Hope

My Portion

The Lord is my portion.

I say to myself, "The LORD is my portion; therefore I will wait for him."

LAMENTATIONS 3:24

I had come to know my friend Meri through the Mommies with Hope support group that I lead. After being married for a year, she and her husband started to try to conceive. It took about two-and-a-half years before Meri became pregnant. She was overjoyed with the pregnancy, but ended up miscarrying in the first trimester. It was an extremely difficult time.

Meri and her husband tried to conceive again, longing for a child to birth and raise on this earth, but month after month, the pregnancy test read negative. With the help of fertility treatments, Meri was able to conceive about a year and a half after her miscarriage. Understandably, it took time before she was able to truly embrace the pregnancy and share the news with others. She had been on this road to motherhood for years, much of that time spent waiting upon the Lord.

Not all of us have had to experience the waiting that Meri did, while others of us have had to wait longer. The point is this: as we wait upon the Lord, may He alone be our portion. I recall moments of my pregnancy with Aiyana where I was so totally consumed by the pregnancy itself that I failed to recognize the Creator as all-sufficient. Wherever you are today and whatever the journey you've traveled that has gotten you to this place, wait upon the Lord with gladness and recognize that He is everything you need.

Dear Lord, You alone are my portion. Help me to keep my eyes fixed on You in all things. I ask that You give me a sense of overwhelming peace during this time. I admit that so often I look to people and things for fulfillment when I need peace, but what I really need is You, God. Help me see that You are enough, always, and that I can trust in You now as I await the birth of my baby. It's in Your precious and all-sufficient name I pray. Amen.

pen the promise

How has the Lord been your portion in the past? How is He your portion in the present? Reflect upon these questions and write your responses in your journal.

I Am Secure

The Lord brings security.

LORD, you alone are my portion and my cup; you make my lot secure.

PSALM 16:5

I know you aren't feeling too secure these days, friend. It's been a hard road to get to this place, a roller coaster to say the least. You may not see it now, but trust me when I tell you that the Lord has been with you every step of the way. He will continue to be with you as you continue on this journey. You are safe. None of us can say what the future holds, but one thing is certain—the Lord holds your future.

Not only does He hold it, but He has shaped and fashioned it with the sovereign work of His mighty hands. Every experience you've had up to this point was divinely orchestrated and allowed by Him for a purpose greater than you or I will ever know this side of heaven. The child you've lost is safe in His arms, literally, while the child you carry within is safe in Him, too.

You don't have to be afraid, friend. As the psalmist says in this key verse, the Lord *alone* is his portion. The Lord makes his lot secure. The same truth that rings true for the psalmist remains true for you and me today. The Lord is our portion—He is all we need. Cling to Him today and trust Him with your tomorrow. You are secure in Him.

Heavenly Father, You make my lot secure. You alone are my portion. Thank You for Your loving care over every aspect of my life, Lord God. When fears and worries seize my day, help me to refocus and realign my thinking to thoughts of You. I want to live in full surrender to You, Jesus. May You alone be all that I need. Amen.

pen the promise ————————————————

In our key verse, the psalmist wrote, "LORD, you alone are my portion." What is your reaction to this statement? Can you say this is true for yourself?

Enduring Provision

God provides a way to endure.

And let us run with perseverance the race marked out for us, fixing our eyes on Jesus, the pioneer and perfecter of faith.

HEBREWS 12:1–2

You will get through this. By God's grace, you will endure. There will be sleepless nights and days of wandering. There will be heart-racing moments of anticipation and moments of absolute dread. There will be times of bittersweet remembering and sweet times of expectation. There will be grief and joy, sorrow overwhelming and peace overflowing, as you continue to walk forward day by day. You will be fine one moment and broken the next, but through everything, God is faithful. He provides a way for you to endure it all.

Provision is found in the Prince of Peace, our Savior Jesus Christ. He is by your side every step of the way; every prenatal appointment, every flit and flutter within. He is there, friend. With a believing heart, place your confidence in His enduring provision for you and for your little one whom you are carrying. He is with you, He is for you, and He goes on before you to make straight the path. Just keep following Him.

Dear Lord, thank You for being my strength in times when I feel as though I don't have the strength to endure one more day. Your Word assures me that I will not have to go through any experience where You are not there and do not provide a way of escape or the ability to endure. Help me, Lord, to see my situation in light of this truth. Help me to never forget the key to enduring—Your Son Jesus. Give me faith to believe and grab hold of this very great and precious promise. In Jesus' name I pray. Amen.

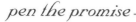 *pen the promise* ———————————————

Is there something about your experience that seems absolutely unbearable? In what ways can you allow Jesus to be your strength and help you endure?

6

The Promise of His Strength

peace in the promise ————————————————

I can do all this through him [Jesus] who gives me strength.

PHILIPPIANS 4:13

You're so strong. This is a "compliment" that I've grown to despise. I've heard it countless times, and I imagine you have, too. After all, what brings us together here amidst these pages is our shared experience of loss and pregnancy thereafter. There's nothing wrong about the phrase, necessarily . . . besides everything about it. At the risk of sounding like a drama queen, I wasn't strong. I'm not strong. Truth be told, I was (and am) a mess most days. I'm emotional and tightly wound and weak in so many ways. And I'm also okay with that. As emotional as I may be and as much as I wrestle with the need to control the uncontrollable—like the knitting together of little ones within my womb—I recognize the fact that it's all in God's hands. Yes, I need reminders (and lots of them), and that is why I cling so tightly to His Word. Jesus, who is the Word (John 1:1), is my strength, and He never fails. He holds all things together (Col. 1:17), including my sanity.

The apostle Paul spoke my heart when He wrote:

Therefore I will boast all the more gladly about my weaknesses, so that Christ's power may rest on me. That is why, for Christ's sake, I delight in weaknesses, in insults, in hardships, in persecutions, in difficulties. For when I am weak, then I am strong. (2 Cor. 12:9–10)

I realize that my weaknesses allow me to rely in greater dependence on Jesus, who is my strength. I need Him every single moment of every day, through every trial and every joyful occasion. Yes, when I'm weak, I'm strong. Not because of anything great about me, but because of He who is in me. Earlier in his second letter to the Corinthians, Paul wrote, "Indeed, we felt we had received the sentence of death. But this happened that we might not rely on ourselves but on God, who raises the dead" (2 Cor. 1:9).

It may be a bit extreme to suggest that pregnancy after loss is a "death sentence." But if we are honest, we wonder and we worry about whether the pregnancy will end in the death of our unborn child once again. The thought of experiencing loss again elicits feelings of dread. We need strength to endure not only the grief, which will forever be a part of our lives, but also these nine months of pregnancy wrought with a vast array of conflicting emotions. After all, women who have a history of loss tend to have a dismal outlook on future pregnancies.

I asked a group of women who experienced pregnancy after loss about their experiences, and many talked about the disconnection they felt, often a result of their own efforts. Jessica so powerfully stated, "I didn't want to let myself fall in love with another baby before it was in my arms. I felt like my womb was a grave, never knowing if life would come from there again." What a difficult place to be parked during pregnancy, a time that for many is filled with awe and wonder and eager excitement. Sometimes the pain of what's happened in the past is too much to bear. It's easier to view things negatively, rather than claim a hopeful view of what's to come.

The good news in all this is that you don't have to be strong in and through all this crazy mix of emotions because God is strong for you. But will you allow Him to be your strength? Or will you try to do this hard thing in your own strength? That is a mistake that I have made more times than I care to admit. You may be able to bear it for a little while, but eventually you will run out of steam and be left exhausted and depleted.

Maybe (probably) you're a bit wiser than me and already realize you can't do it on your own. But you rely primarily on the strength, expertise, and/or help of other people: doctors and medicine; your husband or some other significant person in your life; or the advice given through books, blogs, or articles. Yet all of these resources are just as frail as we are. These things can be wonderful and helpful and perhaps even a bit necessary, but when they become *primary* in our lives, they take the place of the One who was intended to be our true source of strength. Jesus beckons each and every one of us with an invitation to let Him carry the burden. He wants to be *primary*. He must take first place. Jesus longs to give you rest.

peace in the promise ———————————————

"Come to me, all you who are weary and burdened, and I will give you rest."

MATTHEW 11:28

Are You Weary?

"I was weary from worry." Honest words from a sweet mother, Jessica, as she recalled her pregnancy experience with twins. Jessica had two babies on earth and two babies in heaven at the time of her most recent pregnancy with twins. She shared words that I think many of us can relate to:

What if we lost one? Both? What if they both had severe disabilities? I felt so selfish for asking for more kids, knowing the risks. I was weary in my heart from having to know the worst-case scenarios [and having] to prepare for the worst, all the while hoping for the best. I was weary from putting on a show for others—looking like I was happy, worry-free, relying on God—when I was scared, sad, worried, and hanging by a thread of sanity.

Can you relate to the weariness that Jessica described? I sure can. After all, for the woman who is pregnant after loss, it's more than a physical endeavor. It's mental, emotional, and spiritual—sometimes in the worst way as thoughts, feelings, and questions cause you to wonder and wander far from what you know to be true.

There may be real and valid physical weariness that sets in during pregnancy. Jessica was carrying twins who were diagnosed with twin-to-twin transfusion syndrome (TTTS). This situation brought about all kinds of medical questions, concerns, and risks, and resulted in her being placed on bed rest for twelve weeks. It is understandable that a woman in this situation would be weary. Yet the weariness Jessica describes is one of the mind. In a way, the physical and medical challenges exacerbated the mental and spiritual challenges that would later ensue. Pregnancy after loss is accompanied by all sorts of worries, as you well know. Add the complexities of a serious prenatal diagnosis and twelve weeks of idle time, and it's simple to grasp how a woman becomes weary physically, emotionally, spiritually, and mentally.

The same can be said for another mother, Holly. Because of her spinal disease, she experienced great weariness during her pregnancy with her daughter. The physical weariness gave birth to all sorts of mental, emotional, and spiritual weariness. Holly admitted, "Even up to a couple of weeks before my daughter was due, I would have quit if given the chance." It's not that she didn't want her daughter or regretted becoming pregnant again. By no means! It's the pain that accompanied her pregnancy that made her body weary, resulting in thoughts of escape. Holly went on to say:

I'm embarrassed of my feelings and thoughts, but I also know that the Devil delights in feeding me guilt. I think that often one of the hardest things for us, as mothers who have experienced the loss of a child(ren), [is] we feel we must be perfect moms forever and always, because we wanted this sooo bad. We need to give ourselves grace to be human.

There's so much truth to her words. We place undue pressure on ourselves in so many areas, particularly motherhood, and if we're honest, it's our own expectations that lead us to a place of weariness. Truly, Satan wants nothing more than to lead us as far away from the truth as possible. Jesus identified him as the father of lies (John 8:44). First Peter 5:7–9 tells us:

Cast all your anxiety on him [Jesus] because he cares for you.
Be alert and of sober mind. Your enemy the devil prowls around like a roaring lion looking for someone to devour. Resist him, standing firm in the faith, because you know that the family of believers throughout the world is undergoing the same kind of sufferings.

It's unnerving to think about Satan prowling around, looking for whom he will devour next. As the father of lies, he attacks us fiercely through our thoughts. Many times, this is where we are weary. When we are weary—physically, emotionally, mentally—where do we turn for help?

peace in the promise —————————————————

My soul is weary with sorrow, strengthen me according to your word.

PSALM 119:28

_____

According to Your Word

I've tried to go it alone with many things in life—both before knowing Jesus and regrettably even after. Some may chalk it up to my personality, my stubbornness, or my strong will and determination. At times, my initiative and my independence can be a positive characteristic or quality. It's this mind-set that allows me to excel in various areas of life. But when initiative and independence take on the form of control, that's a whole different ball game. As a follower of Christ, I ought to be in constant surrender to His leading in my life. When trials come, when anxiety wells up, and when fears threaten to consume, I need to press in all the more closely to my Savior and entrust Him with every burden. When I attempt to shoulder the burdens on my own, I may "succeed" for a time, but before too long I will succumb to the weariness. Contrastingly—and perhaps even more detrimentally—when I take too much credit for the joys and blessings in my life, I neglect seeing the holy hand of my Sovereign Lord at work on my behalf and begin to take His blessings for granted. Either end of the spectrum is a dangerous place to be. How, then, do we come to a healthy balance and glean our strength from God? *By His Word.*

Just as our peace-in-the-promise verse states above, we receive strength from His Word. When our souls are weary with sorrow, He strengthens us by His Word. In times of rejoicing, we also need His Word. Psalm 119, the longest psalm and the longest chapter in the entire Bible, encompasses 176 verses where the psalmist declares the utmost significance of God's Word. According to the psalmist, God's Word brings delight, preserves, strengthens, sustains, stands firm, is filled with promise, gives hope, brings salvation, and brings peace. I

Expecting with Hope

encourage you to take some time to read Psalm 119. Ask the Lord to open your heart and allow you to take on the perspective of the psalmist, who clearly had a tremendous love and reverence for God's Word. No matter where you are spiritually, spending some time pouring over this psalm will bring wonderful insight as to how God's Word can and will give you strength for the journey.

In the New Testament, we learn that "all Scripture is God-breathed and is useful for teaching, rebuking, correcting and training in righteousness, so that the servant of God may be thoroughly equipped for every good work" (2 Tim. 3:16–17). The Bible is more than a mere collection of books *about* God. The Bible is breathed out by God Himself to teach, correct, train, and equip us. It's not some ancient text that was suitable for a time in history. It is a collection of the words of the author of history itself. It was relevant then, and it is relevant now. Hebrews 4:12 reads, "For the word of God is alive and active. Sharper than any double-edged sword, it penetrates even to dividing soul and spirit, joints and marrow; it judges the thoughts and attitudes of the heart." How can the Word of God be alive and active? For one, because Jesus is the Word, and Jesus is alive! That's the good news of the gospel. That is why He is the Prince of Peace who brings peace to our hearts and to our circumstances. We can trust in the living Word because we have a living hope in the resurrected Christ!

After digging into the Word to learn a bit about God's Word, the question remains: Are you in the Word yourself? Do you love God's Word, rely on it, look to it to guide and direct your path? The responses to these questions will probably cover the spectrum. For some, reading this book may be the first time you've read anything from the Bible. For others, you may have read the entire Bible multiple times. For many of us who are meeting within the context of these pages, the Bible contains value of some sort and we are working to integrate God's Word into our lives. Whatever the case, God desires to know you and for you to know Him, made possible through His Word. If you don't know where to start, I would encourage you to do two things: First, read one chapter in Proverbs each day. It has thirty-one chapters, so there's one chapter for each day of most months. Secondly, read the gospel of John, which will teach you more about the life and teachings of Jesus, our source of all hope and strength, our precious Prince of Peace. Before you open God's Word, simply ask Him to reveal those truths and promises that He wants you to know and embrace. Consider praying these words of Samuel: "Speak, for your servant is listening" (1 Sam. 3:10). Be encouraged by this beautiful analogy contained in Isaiah 55:10–11, where the Lord God says:

> As the rain and the snow come down from heaven, and do not return to it without watering the earth and making it bud and flourish, so that it yields seed for the sower and bread for the eater, so is my word that goes out from my mouth: It will not return to me empty, but will accomplish what I desire and achieve the purpose for which I sent it.

You Can Do It!

The feat may seem insurmountable, but in Christ you can do all things. I don't have to know you to recognize that you are brave, sweet friend. You may be thinking, *Really? What does she know?* I realize you may not *feel* brave. Perhaps me telling you that you are is akin to people telling me, "You're so strong," which, as you know, I don't like. But listen, my friend: you are brave because you have displayed great courage. You've survived the deep hurt of losing a child and now courageously persevere in pregnancy once again, despite a painful past and without assurance of the outcome. One must be brave to endure. To the outsiders you look "so strong," but strength alone doesn't account for the fact that you are willing to face your fear of what *could* happen again as you await the arrival of your little one. Strength by the world's standards means we are able to withstand pressure and force without being broken. The truth is that grief breaks us down to the very core; so much so that we realize how weak we truly are and how desperately we need Jesus. Remember the words of the apostle Paul, "For when I am weak, then I am strong" (2 Cor. 12:10).

I'm not suggesting that you or I have done things perfectly or "right" because, truly, there's really no right way to do this crazy thing called grief. Still, we are brave, you and I both. We survived loss and we continue to survive and thrive, even on the darkest days. The intensity of the grief will wane, but grief will be a constant companion of sorts as we continue to settle into a new normal, a part of which means the welcoming home of more children, Lord willing.

You can do this. You *are* doing this. I urge you, claim joy now. Claim victory today. Sink in to the shelter of the Lord God, who is your strength. If you wait until your baby arrives safe and sound—which I imagine is the absolute longing of your heart—you miss out on so much of this precious and sacred time of carrying your child in the womb. These days are numbered, and you cannot reclaim them. Your child's life began the moment he or she was conceived all those weeks or months ago. Your child is your child *now.*

When Jessica recalled her pregnancy after the loss of Elihu at fifteen weeks along, she put up a guard around her heart. She was still grieving the loss of Elihu when she became pregnant. Ten weeks into the pregnancy, a sweet baby that she and her husband named Elliot joined Elihu in heaven. Jessica reflected on her miscarriage of her baby after the loss of Elihu:

> My biggest regret was not letting myself fall in love with Elliot. Falling in love hurt, and I thought that [keeping myself from that] would be the best way to guard my heart, but that's not true. I felt guilty. I felt like I didn't really know this little person, and I grieved with guilt.

I hate to consider the possibility of multiple losses, but I would be remiss not to acknowledge that sometimes subsequent pregnancies do end in loss. My own sweet Jesse and Riyah Mae were both children conceived after Chloe had died, yet after the healthy birth of Aiyana. I am keenly aware of this experience. While it is absolutely my deepest desire and prayer for you and the baby who grows within that your pregnancy will progress and result in your baby being born alive and well, I can't make that guarantee.

But I can share insight from my own experience and from women like Jessica to encourage you to be strong in the Lord now. Get to know your child now. Don't even attempt to build those walls around your heart, because the truth is that this sweet baby not only occupies your womb, but the love you have for him or her consumes your heart, as much as you may try to deny it. Enjoy this time, cherish these moments, and don't waste a single second more with worrying yourself into a state of debilitating weariness. Instead, stand firm in the truth that you can do all things through Christ, who gives you strength (Phil. 4:13).

My Pregnancy Prayer for You

God Almighty, we need Your strength. I pray, Lord, that You would grace this precious woman with a strength that can only come from You and from knowing You. Lord, I pray that she would know You in a real and personal way. Give her faith to believe that You are mighty to save. Help her to combat lies with truth and to be seeking You in all things. As she dives into Your strength-giving Word, I pray that You would reveal Your promises, that You would help her to persevere, and that by relying on Your precious Word, You would bring her peace. Amen.

Expecting with Hope

All Things Through Christ

Jesus gives strength.

I can do all this through him [Christ] who gives me strength.

PHILIPPIANS 4:13

In the weeks and months after Chloe died, I wasn't sure I'd ever want to have more children. Not because I didn't have a desire for more, but because I didn't think I would have the strength to endure the *possibility* of another loss. I had learned firsthand that pregnancy doesn't always result in a full-term, healthy baby, as I had once naïvely believed. In fact, at our six-week postpartum appointment, I remember the nurse practitioner asking us what our plans were for contraception, and I jokingly (though somewhat seriously) replied, "Abstinence," in my attempt to steer clear of the chance of even becoming pregnant. It was all too scary, and in a way I was right; I didn't have the strength to face any of those possibilities.

Over the months, and as we approached the one-year anniversary of Chloe's birth and death, the Lord began softening my heart to the idea of more children, and I realized that I didn't have to do any of this in my own strength. After all, I had been learning so well to rely on His strength to see me through those hard days of my grief journey. Should we become pregnant again—and whether or not the baby was born alive and healthy—His strength could certainly sustain me. It was His strength that saw me through the pregnancy and birth of my daughter, Aiyana, and the subsequent miscarriages of sweet Jesse and Riyah Mae.

Christ's strength is limitless. The same strength that He offered to me then and continues to offer to me now, is available to you. In Christ, you can do all things. You can face the pain of your past, the trepidation of your today, and the fear of your future with great hope and reliance on Him to daily bear your burdens. Let Him be your strength, one day at a time.

Dear Lord, I need You to be my strength. In You, Jesus, I can do all things—things that from my human perspective seem downright impossible. But I know from Your Word that all things are possible with God. Help me to rely upon You and You alone to be my ultimate source of strength. It's in Your strong name I pray. Amen.

pen the promise ─────────────────────

Think of a time when you gained strength from Jesus and write about it in your journal. In what areas of your life do you need to ask Him to be your strength today?

When I'm Weak, I'm Strong

pregnancy promise ————————————————————

Jesus' grace is sufficient.

But he said to me, "My grace is sufficient for you, for my power is made perfect in weakness." Therefore I will boast all the more gladly about my weaknesses, so that Christ's power may rest on me. That is why, for Christ's sake, I delight in weaknesses, in insults, in hardships, in persecutions, in difficulties. For when I am weak, then I am strong.

2 CORINTHIANS 12:9–10

Good news, friend. You don't have to be strong. I know this world has been sending the message to you ever since your loss(es) that "you are so strong." It's a message you've believed and probably one you've come to expect of yourself. Now that you are pregnant again, you think, *I should be okay.* After all, that's what others seem to be communicating to you; others whom you trust and respect. Surely, they must be right.

Give yourself permission to not *be* anything but you. Some days you will feel "strong" and other days you will feel as though you could melt into a puddle on the floor. On those days, have a piece of chocolate and blame it on the hormones. In all seriousness, each and every day press in closer and closer to Jesus, who longs to be your strength.

While the world may value what they perceive to be strength, God's Word gives permission for us to show weakness. In fact, it encourages weakness. According to our key verse, Christ's power is made perfect in weakness. The apostle Paul wrote that when he was weak, he was strong. This is possible because Jesus' grace carries us through. Jesus is enough and He is all-sufficient. He is ready, willing, and able to see us through every one of life's trials and blessings. So be weak, friend, because in Christ you are strong.

Dear Lord, thank You for showing me that I don't have to be strong. I admit that I have often put this pressure on myself, and it's exhausting. Help me to always see that You are more than strong enough to carry me through. Help me to always understand that weakness really means strength as I place my full trust in You. Protect me from the messages of this world and the pressure I've placed upon myself to "be strong," and help me to see that You, Jesus, are more than enough! Amen.

pen the promise ———————————————————————

In what ways have you felt pressured to be strong during your pregnancy? Write about your experiences in your journal.

My Strength

The Lord is my strength.

I love you, LORD, my strength.

PSALM 18:1

Along this journey are times—some of which you have probably already experienced—when you can't come up with the words to even begin to describe how you feel. You're weak, you're confused by your emotions, and you are downright tired. I experienced those moments in my own journey of pregnancy after loss, and quite honestly, still experience them in other areas of life. When I don't know how to pray, what to say, or what to do, I call to mind this short, yet powerful, key verse and pray it to God.

I say this verse repeatedly, *"I love you, LORD, my strength. I love you, LORD, my strength."* Sometimes the tears flow, and I cry and catch my breath. Eventually the tears subside and I breathe in more of Jesus, more of His grace, and a strength that can only come from Him overwhelms me.

What about you? As you travel this journey of pregnancy after loss, consider the areas of this experience where you need to rely on the strength that only God can provide. Perhaps you need strength to wrestle through the many emotions of grief that are very much a part of your everyday life. You may also need strength for the physical fatigue and weariness of your body as you work hard to carry another little one within. More than likely, it's the difficult combination of both of these areas and more. Whatever your need, may you continually surrender to the loving grace of our Lord, who gives you strength.

Dear heavenly Father, You are a God of great strength. Help me to rely on You to be my strength in and through all things. I pray, Lord, that You would be my strength today and every day. Help me to know Your great love and to respond with love in return. Give me great faith with a spirit that is humbled before You and continually looking to You for strength. When days are long, emotions run high, and pains cut deep, be my strength. Amen.

pen the promise ────────────────────

Meditate on the key verse above and write it in your journal. Reflect upon this verse and write a prayer to God based on your meditations.

Strong in Grace

pregnancy promise ────────────────────

The grace of Jesus gives strength.

You then, my son, be strong in the grace that is in Christ Jesus.

2 TIMOTHY 2:1

The grace of God found in our Lord Jesus Christ is a free gift to all who believe. *Grace* defined is "unmerited favor." In other words, there is nothing that we can do to earn it. Ephesians 2:8–9 explains, "For it is by grace you have been saved, through faith—and this is not from yourselves, it is the gift of God." Grace is a gift that God chooses to lovingly lavish upon us. This extension of grace was offered by the sacrifice that Jesus made on the cross of Calvary. When we know the Prince of Peace, it is this act of grace that rescues us from our own sin and spiritual death. In our key verse, Paul is instructing Timothy to "be strong in the grace that is in Christ Jesus"—this same saving grace that was displayed on the cross.

Such amazing grace is too magnificent to fully comprehend. It's mind-boggling that God would freely offer such an amazing gift. Just as great as the gift of grace is the strength that we can have in Christ because of such grace. We can be strong in the grace of Jesus, because of the strength that Jesus displays and provides. Therefore, dear friend, when you are feeling weak, weary, and plain worn out, call to mind the amazing grace that is in Christ Jesus. Persevere and carry on with grace by the power of His mighty name.

Dear Lord, Your grace is amazing. It's hard to fathom how deeply You love us and that You would choose to lavish such grace upon us. Lord, I need Your grace to sustain me. I pray that in the mighty name of Jesus

You would give me strength to face the day. Help me walk forward with confidence, and remind me of Your truth when I need to hear it. Jesus, You are full of grace, and I thank You for loving me so. Amen.

pen the promise ───────────────

Think of a time when God's grace was apparent to you in your life or circumstances. How did such awareness change your perspective or give you strength?

Weary

Give your weariness to God.

"I am weary, God, but I can prevail."

PROVERBS 30:1

Pregnancy, in and of itself, brings about weariness in a woman. After all, your body is doing the physical work of growing and nurturing another human being! We tend to lose sight of this fact and to take the miracle of pregnancy and childbirth for granted. In addition to the expected fatigue that comes along with pregnancy, a spiritual and emotional weariness can accompany pregnancy after loss.

Sandy shared a story with me about weariness in her pregnancy with her daughter, Teagan. Her husband was working out of state, so she went to the nineteen-week ultrasound alone, only to be referred to a perinatologist's office for a more detailed exam because they believed that her baby had a heart defect. It appeared that part of the baby's heart hadn't formed. Sandy had to wait five more weeks before going in for the more in-depth ultrasound in order to give her baby more time to grow and so that the doctor could see her heart more clearly. Sandy recalled the experience and said:

[It was the] longest five weeks ever, and we told nobody. At that ultrasound, I was told her heart was developed, but again, there appeared to be a defect, or it was Down syndrome. I could have [had] an amnio, but it was risky given my second-trimester losses due to preterm labor. We chose to just wait and trust. . . . Boy, that was hard! Every day I felt like I was just a weary soul asking—no, pleading—with God to just let my baby live and stay here with us on earth. Every day, until one day around thirty-three weeks when I just finally said I couldn't drag myself around like this. I started praying instead for peace in my weary heart.

Three weeks later, Teagan was born, free from any heart defect or any other suspected health complications.

When you are feeling weary, speak aloud the words of the psalmist: "I am weary, God, but I can prevail." Do not merely speak these words, but believe them. Claim them as your own. Trust in God, that by His strength, you will prevail despite all weariness.

Dear God, You are the mighty Creator. As my precious baby grows within me, I ask that You would give me strength to prevail, even on the most weary of days. Give me physical energy, as well as the emotional and spiritual energy to stay focused on You and Your exceedingly great and precious promises. In You, Lord, I know I will prevail! Amen.

pen the promise ———————————————————

In what ways are you weary: Physically? Emotionally? Spiritually? Write a prayer to God asking Him for strength in these areas.

Expecting with Hope

The Promise of Contentment in Him

peace in the promise ————————————————

For I have learned to be content whatever the circumstances. . . . I have learned the secret of being content in any and every situation.

PHILIPPIANS 4:11–12

Through my own loss experiences, one thing I have learned is the painful sting of hearing other women complain about anything related to pregnancy and children—the symptoms, the discomfort, the sleepless nights from nursing, and the demands of parenthood. These complaints feel like salt to the wound for the woman who is missing a baby who has died or is longing for a baby.

Sad to say, I have been on the complaining end of the spectrum, as well. I've felt (and voiced) discontent at my two living children's inability to get along. I can't count how many times in a day I find myself saying some variation of "Please be kind to one another!" It's embarrassing to admit, but I've even allowed my thoughts to take me down the path of resentment, wondering if things would be different in our family had my other children lived. There wouldn't be a six-year age gap between the two, and the dynamics would surely be better, I convince myself, further contributing to my discontent.

After I wallow in self-pity for a time, I bring myself back to what I know to be true—God's Word and His promises—and check my attitude. When I fall into a pit of discontentment, it's usually because I'm basing my joy on my circumstances. In all actuality, true joy comes not from having two feet planted firmly in the Promised Land, but from resting in the promises of God as we journey through the ups and downs of life. As you take inventory in your life, I imagine there are many situations, past and present, that could become a major source of discontent. If we park ourselves in those places for too long, we run the risk of falling into all sorts of sin—with envy and bitterness at the forefront. How do you think our attitudes might change if we stopped focusing on everything *wrong* in our world, and instead focused on all that is *right*?

In our peace-in-the-promise verse, the apostle Paul confidently claimed that he has learned to be content in all circumstances. Really? *All* circumstances? What's his secret?

What's the Secret?

Paul's secret was nothing more nor less than a genuine faith in Jesus Christ. If we're honest, many of us probably claim to have such a faith, yet we fail in the area of contentment. Someone else always has it better. From material things to relationships, we always want what we don't have. That, my friend, is evidence of discontentment in our lives. And to put it plainly, it's sin. When we wish our lives could be just the way so-and-so has it—we are coveting our neighbor (Exod. 20:17). If we take this a step further and examine whether our loss experiences, our attempts to bear children, or our current pregnancy have consumed us and conclude that they have, then we are breaking

God's command that we shall have no other gods before Him (Exod. 20:3). We've fallen into idolatry and worshipped something or someone other than God Himself.

My friend and fellow pregnancy-after-loss mom Meri shared her perspective on contentment this way:

> Contentment is the magical unicorn that I have always been chasing. It's always been, after _____ (fill in the blank), I will be content. . . . Sadly, contentment eluded me. I am so happy with Johanna [her daughter born after loss], but discontented that I have to put her in daycare when I want to stay home with her. So contentment eludes me yet again.

We are not unlike Meri. In our humanness, we all do this. We continually chase after what we expect will provide contentment and the ultimate satisfaction. Obtaining the object of our striving may satisfy for a moment, but the pleasure is fleeting when it is rooted in the frailty of people or things. There will always be something more that we continue to chase after.

Jessica shared her experience with discontentment during her pregnancy with twins after two pregnancy losses:

> I was happy to be pregnant again, but to have fear looming over me made me wish for more. To have complications with the twins [whom I had] begged God for made me disappointed, and I wanted more. I have to admit that I was discontent while on bed rest. I didn't want this package, God. I wanted more. I wanted easy. I wanted healthy. I wanted what I wanted, and I wanted it my way. I wanted to be able to be naïve again. To enjoy pregnancy without fear.

Jessica shared a laundry list of issues that brought about discontentment, but at the end of the day, it all boils down to her final statement: "[I want] to enjoy pregnancy without fear." I imagine you can relate. I sure can. I think back to my pregnancies after Chloe died, and I longed for freedom from fear, anxiety, and worry. But pregnancy will never be the same.

Another pregnancy-after-loss mother, LeeAnn, conveyed this so clearly: "When you have known loss once or multiple times, you never see things that involve pregnancy the same again." She's right. Everything is different.

If you are in a place of wanting more or have feelings of discontent, please know that you're not alone. Many have walked this path of pregnancy after loss and struggle with discontent, only to let guilt and shame consume them as they tell themselves, "I should be so thankful for this healthy baby growing within me." Perhaps. It's one thing to know that deep down, but it's another to truly live as though you believe it. In doing so, you may feel as though you are invalidating the very real presence of lingering grief over your baby in heaven. Besides, it's impossible to deny the reality that not every baby survives pregnancy and childbirth the way we once naïvely thought.

Nichelle, a dear friend and a facilitator of one of the Mommies with Hope support groups (appendix D), has had quite the journey to motherhood. She's struggled with infertility, miscarriage, and the death of her stillborn son, Eli. As Nichelle recalled her pregnancy-after-loss experiences, she said:

> Contentment and perspective went hand in hand . . . united as one. When I started to feel discontentment, I looked at the hardship of others. No matter what your struggle or grief, there is always someone who is suffering more. . . . [I mean this] in no way as a competition. Perspective brought contentment in His will not mine.

Nichelle's point made me pause and think about the connection of contentment and perspective. She's right in saying that there is no competition, because suffering is suffering. My trial may not look the same as the next person's, but trials are trials. That being said, viewing our circumstances in perspective helps us to see that there is much to be grateful for, even amid the uncertainty and anticipation. You may be so overwhelmed by your circumstances today that it seems impossible to view your pregnancy after loss in any different light than you are using right this very moment. Especially at such times, it's imperative that we ask the Lord to show us our situation in light of Him. On our own, it may be possible to find contentment in the moment, but with God we are able not only to find fleeting moments of contentment, but to live contentedly for the long term, as well.

peace in the promise ———————————

"So I [Jesus] say to you: Ask and it will be given to you; seek and you will find; knock and the door will be opened to you."

LUKE 11:9

Seek and Ye Shall Find

Finding contentment is not too difficult; staying there is a whole other story. We can be content for a little while with just about anything. Living in a perpetual state of contentment takes intentional, deliberate, and meaningful perspective shifting and prayer. Our peace-in-the-promise verse tells us plainly to ask, seek, and find. In context, this verse directly follows the instructions Jesus gives to the disciples on how to pray, commonly known as the Lord's Prayer. Jesus is telling us to come to Him, to seek Him, and to ask. If we are lacking in the area of contentment, let us go to God in prayer and ask for it. Let me be clear: by *it* I mean contentment itself, not the object or event that we believe will bring us contentment.

For example, I mentioned at the beginning of this chapter my current struggle with my children's treatment of one another. It's an area that brings me discontent, which is difficult to admit because I certainly am grateful for these two living miracles! So often my prayers are for intervention or a plea for change. That's not all bad, but when I take a closer look, what I'm really praying is for the Lord to change them. I want *them* to get along. I want *them* to be kind. I want *them* to be patient and loving. But if I'm going to pray for change, my prayers ought to be more along these lines: Lord, change *me*. Help *me* to be content and not resentful. Start with *me*.

When we seek God with our whole hearts, He promises to be found (Jer. 29:13). When we find Him, know Him, and get to know Him more, our desires change. Sure, we still want what we want. Ultimately though, we long to please Him. Our desires change in a way that aligns with His good and perfect will for our lives. We're able to look at our trials with the confidence that God knows what He's doing. Like the wife of noble character described in Proverbs 31, we can "laugh at the days to come" (v. 25). We laugh not out of humor but out of confidence. We are not consumed by fear and anxiety over what may or may not be. We know that Jesus is enough. At the end of the day, Jesus has to be enough.

peace in the promise ————————————————

But he said to me, "My grace is sufficient for you, for my power is made perfect in weakness."

2 CORINTHIANS 12:9

Sufficient Grace

What does it mean, exactly, that Jesus has to be enough? Simply stated, it means that our source of contentment comes from knowing Him as Savior and Lord of our lives. If our contentment is based on circumstances rather than our Savior, we will continually experience discontented lives. In Paul's second letter to the Corinthians, he explains a vision that he had and goes on to describe a thorn in his flesh. Here's what he had to say about it:

> Therefore, in order to keep me from becoming conceited, I was given a thorn in my flesh, a messenger of Satan, to torment me. Three times I pleaded with the LORD to take it away from me. But he said to me, "My grace is sufficient for you, for my power is made perfect in weakness." Therefore I will boast all the more gladly about my weaknesses, so that Christ's power may rest on me. That is why, for Christ's sake, I delight in weaknesses, in insults, in hardships, in persecutions, in difficulties. For when I am weak, then I am strong. (2 Cor. 12:7–10)

Each of our "thorns" will look different, and some of us may have several to contend with. We can all agree that the cup of grief we've shared has been difficult. Some of you may be pregnant now after years of infertility, multiple losses, or the use of assistive reproductive technologies. Whatever the case, we can—like Paul—choose to see that in our weakness, Christ's power is at work. We can ask the Lord to remove the thorn, but maybe the thorn is the very thing that keeps us seeking after Jesus with our whole heart. In our weaknesses we are strong, as we delight in Him and Him alone.

As I was talking with some ladies who've been through the experience of pregnancy after loss about this matter of Jesus being enough, Kim recollected her childbearing years and admitted that she seemed to rely on God more through the experience of losing her daughter, Gabrielle, and less with her two subsequent pregnancies. Medically, things were going well. She recalled, "I knew God was there, but I didn't think about it as much." Kim's candid response caused me to think about situations in my own life. I have to admit that there have been times when things were going smoothly and life was going well, so I had less of a regard for the Lord than during times of crisis. When I was in crisis mode, I realized just how much I absolutely need Him.

The truth is we need Him every single moment of every single day; whether we are on a mountaintop high or deep-in-the-valley low. In times of rejoicing and in times of sorrow, Jesus and only Jesus has to be enough.

Cultivating Contentment

How, then, do we cultivate a climate of contentment when our circumstances beg us to dwell in the land of discontent? It's a valid question—one I've had to really think and pray through myself as I've struggled with discontent. The first thing is to identify areas of discontent and call them as they are. I realize that a sense of entitlement may be at play here. Some of these thoughts may be racing through your mind right about now:

> I have every right to be worried.
> I've suffered so much and, therefore, have earned the right to complain.
> I'll never fully be content without my baby(ies) who died.
> I am always left wanting more _____ (peace, satisfaction, children, etc.).
> I won't be content until this baby is born alive and well.
> I don't think it's possible to ever be content in life.

Do any of the above statements resonate with you? It may sting a bit to admit, as I realize they aren't the most pleasant of declarations. More than likely, we wouldn't voice these statements aloud. If we're honest, I imagine that we can all relate to some of them. If we wear the banner of any of these statements for too long, we take on the attitude reflected by the statement itself. We become comfortable. It seems strange to think that one could be comfortable in a state of discontent, yet that's precisely what happens when we fail to do anything about it. Quite honestly, Satan would love to keep us there with his lies. It takes a will of our spirit, a strength from God, and a willingness to change

Expecting with Hope

and be changed to cultivate contentment in our lives. Just because others may echo the above sentiments or because you have girlfriends and relatives validating your state of discontent doesn't mean that that's where the Lord wants you to remain. Romans 12:2 says, "Do not conform to the pattern of this world, but be transformed by the renewing of your mind. Then you will be able to test and approve what God's will is—his good, pleasing and perfect will." Let God and His Word be your guide, not people.

We already know the secret to contentment that Paul speaks of in his letter to the Philippians: the Lord, Jesus Christ. As you seek to grow in your relationship with Him, you can do some very practical things during this time of pregnancy after loss to cultivate a heart of genuine contentment in Christ. Here are just a few ideas to consider:

- *Pray.* Live a life of perpetual prayer. Many reserve prayers solely for meals and bedtime, but prayer can take place anywhere, anytime. If you're not accustomed to praying throughout your day, set reminders and be intentional about carving out time to spend simply talking to God. It's your way of communicating with God and pouring into the relationship. Ask God to show you areas of your life where discontentment rears its ugly head, and ask Him to change you. Go to the Lord with a sincere heart and share your burdens, your praises, and everything in between. Continual prayer will help you to grow in your relationship with God, just as communication with a friend or spouse helps you to grow in your relationship with them.

- *Worship.* We can worship God in many ways, including corporately through a weekly church service, in small group Bible studies, through music that we listen to or sing, and even through giving and serving. Let your acts of worship be an offering to the Lord, and worship Him fully with a pure heart. As you do, you will grow in intimacy with Him. Do not participate in worship begrudgingly, but do so eagerly and with zeal. Pray and ask God to change your heart and attitude so that you may worship Him in the way that He desires you to worship Him.

- *Read and Study the Word.* In chapter 6 we spent quite a bit of time delving into the importance and power of God's Word. Just as prayer is your way of speaking to God, the Bible is one way God speaks to you. In prayer, open His Word and seek to understand His promises. Consider participating in a Bible study in your community or online. By reading and studying God's Word, you will be blessed and begin to see your circumstances in light of God's Holy Word.

- *Practice Gratitude.* It's amazing what the act of giving thanks will do for a person's perspective. Realizing how much we have to be grateful for helps us to put our many burdens and worries into perspective. Count your blessings, literally. Write them down, keep a gratitude journal, write notes of thanks to those special family members and friends who support you in so many wonderful ways. As dark as the days may get, there's always something to be thankful for. And as difficult as it may be to imagine your baby within being born alive and well, pause and thank God for your child's life *today*.

These suggestions are focused entirely on growing in your relationship with God, through Christ. After all, He is the secret to being content in all things. As you work to cultivate contentment, you will naturally seek to please and glorify God with every aspect of your life, including your perspective on this current pregnancy, as frightening as it may be. As a result, you will shine like the stars (Phil. 2:15). Others will look at you and know something is different. They will see your "secret"—Jesus—shining through you.

peace in the promise ————————————————

Do everything without grumbling or arguing, so that you may become blameless and pure, "children of God without fault in a warped and crooked generation." Then you will shine among them like stars in the sky as you hold firmly to the word of life.

PHILIPPIANS 2:14–16

My Pregnancy Prayer for You

Dear Lord, You are all-sufficient. Help us to live in the light of this absolute truth. May You always take first place in our lives. Jesus, I pray that You would be with the woman who is reading this and help her to see that true contentment, true satisfaction is found in You alone. Let the striving cease, Lord, and may her joy be in You alone. Help her to recognize the many blessings that You provide, and give her perspective. Give her a spirit like that of Paul, who was confident in the secret to being content in all things: that secret being You, Jesus. Amen.

Focus on the Truth

pregnancy promise ————————————————

Focus, always, on the truth.
Finally, brothers and sisters, whatever is true, whatever is noble, whatever is right, whatever is pure, whatever is lovely, whatever is admirable—if anything is excellent or praiseworthy—think about such things.

PHILIPPIANS 4:8

Our thoughts have a tendency to run rampant if we let them. We overanalyze and travel on autopilot to the absolute worst-case scenario, particularly if we've experienced the worst before. Thoughts can consume us if we aren't careful, causing us to believe things that simply are not true. I asked some women who've experienced loss about some of the thoughts that went through their minds during subsequent pregnancy. One woman, Kristi, shared:

> By the time I was pregnant with my son, I had experienced a chemical pregnancy, a "normal" first-trimester loss, and a second trimester loss. We had begun a ministry to other parents of babies in heaven, and I wondered if God just wanted me to experience a third-trimester loss or infant death, because then I would have the full experience of loss and would be able to minister better. I would not believe that my son would be born alive until he came out crying.

As Kristi shared her heart, I could relate so well, having had those very thoughts myself. Instead of focusing on the very truth set in front of me—that I had a baby growing within, who by all appearances was healthy—I was consumed by overanalysis and worst-case scenarios.

If you are in that place today—focused on the worst instead of the truth—grab hold of this verse from Philippians and examine these words with an open heart and open mind. Be honest as you ask yourself, what is true, what is lovely, what is pure, what is right, excellent, and praiseworthy? Realign your thinking to focus on the truth, rather than on your fears.

Father in heaven, You are lovely. You are excellent; You are worthy of all of my praise. Help me to focus on You. Lord, I pray that by the power of your Holy Spirit You would permeate every one of my thoughts so that I may be focused on the truth. I do not want to be tempted to buy into the lies of what could be or to be consumed by the memories of what has happened. Keep my mind set on things above, Lord, and bring me Your peace. Amen.

pen the promise ————————————————

Copy Philippians 4:8 into your journal. Reflect on this verse and write down what you know to be true about this pregnancy journey. Give praise to God for what is true!

New

God is doing a new thing.

See, I am doing a new thing! Now it springs up; do you not perceive it? I am making a way in the wilderness and streams in the wasteland.

ISAIAH 43:19

I really disliked the attention I got during my pregnancy after loss. People tend to dote over a glowing pregnant woman anyway, but I felt as though people were especially overjoyed that we were going to have a baby after Chloe died. I believe they were genuinely happy for us, but I felt like they somehow believed this pregnancy would be the antidote to my grief. It wasn't. After we found out that we were having another girl, the attention just seemed to increase. People would ask, "Do you know what you're having?" to which I'd succinctly reply, "Yes, we're having a girl." I always hoped it would be left at that, but more often than I care to recall, my simple response would be followed by an overly empathic, "Awwww . . . that is *so good!*" Again, genuinely happy, I am sure. But the message that was conveyed to me was this: "That is so good! Because Chloe was a girl, but she died. So now you can have your perfect little family: a boy and a girl."

I admit there was probably a degree of irrational thinking taking place in my mind when I (mis)perceived others' heartfelt encouragement. Still, I couldn't help but feel as though everyone else viewed my new baby girl as a replacement for my first baby girl. Just because I was having another girl didn't mean that she was replacing my daughter who had died.

I can't say that I mastered the management of these emotions during my pregnancy. It's only in looking back that I can truly see the situation for what it was: friends and loved ones who were genuinely happy for us. Myself? A bit jaded, defensive, and borderline bitter. Yet I knew that God was doing a *new* thing. He was knitting together a different daughter in my womb who would have a different purpose in this life. She'd never be a replacement child, and she'd always be my second daughter. God was also doing a new thing in me—physically and spiritually—as I wrestled with these many mixed emotions. He's doing a new thing in and through you, too.

God, thank You for doing a new thing in me through my pregnancy after loss. You have shown me that Your creation is unique and one of a kind. I praise You for helping me to see that friends and loved ones genuinely care about my journey, even when my own feelings and insecurities get in the way and jade my view. Help me, Lord, to always be on the lookout for the new thing that You desire to do in and through me. I want to follow hard after You always. Amen.

pen the promise —————————————————————

Have you struggled with comparisons between your baby who died and this baby who grows within you now? Write your thoughts in your journal.

Content in Him

pregnancy promise ─────────────────────

You can be content in Jesus, regardless of your circumstances.

And my God will meet all your needs according to the riches of his glory in Christ Jesus.

PHILIPPIANS 4:19

After Alesa experienced the loss of her baby girl, it was hard to hear the well-meaning clichés that people offered up as a form of support. She shared her honest portrayal of how she grew to a place of contentment in Christ, despite the difficulty of her circumstances:

> The first few weeks [after loss] I was very angry with God. I didn't want to hear that He had a plan, I didn't want to hear I would see my sweet girl again in heaven. I wanted her then, and I wanted her *now*. In that first month, I started going to a Bible study through an infant-loss support group. . . . I held onto Jesus and the promise He made. I still have questions but know He is the almighty and has His reasons. Through my subsequent pregnancies, the only thing that I could do [was] trust in the Lord. Whether we lost again or got to keep our babies, I knew God had a plan and I had faith in Him.

Quite often, God uses our most challenging and difficult trials in life to bring us to a place of intimately knowing and growing in Him as a result. While Alesa struggled with questions and anger over her losses, God met her in that place of pain and revealed Himself to her.

Alesa was able to get to a place in her faith where she could honestly say that she trusted in God's plan and had faith in Him, whatever happened. That's the mark of true contentment. God knows our needs completely, and He provides everything we need through Jesus.

Dear God, You are an amazing God who cares deeply for what I am going through. Help me, Lord, to trust in You even when I can't see or know how things will possibly turn out. You know my needs, and I pray for Your provision and for contentment with however You choose to bless me. Thank You for Your Son Jesus, who by His sacrifice has rescued me. It's in His precious name I pray. Amen.

pen the promise ────────────────────────

Write your reaction to Alesa's story. Are you content in Christ, or do you base contentment more upon your circumstances? Write your reflection.

Great Gain

pregnancy promise ─────────────────────

It takes very little for the godly to be content.

But godliness with contentment is great gain.

1 TIMOTHY 6:6

In Paul's first letter to Timothy, he shares some parting wisdom about godliness and contentment, warning Timothy about the dangers of chasing after wealth. According to Paul, food and clothing are what we need, and we ought to be content with those things alone. Let's face it, in our culture we tend to lose sight of what our true needs are. But God's Word is timeless, and the words Paul spoke to Timothy some two thousand years ago are the same words that ring true for us today.

Consequently, it's imperative that we look at these verses with a heart aimed at pleasing God and examining ourselves. Are we truly content? We live in a society of great abundance and blessing. Still, we are continually left wanting *more.* This desire for more is not about things, my friend. It is an issue of the heart.

As you think about your pregnancy, what area of discontent poses a challenge for you now? How have you allowed longing, worry, fear, or other thoughts and feelings to stand in the way of true contentment in God? Paul tells us that godliness with contentment is great gain. Therefore, we ought to be living our lives in a godly way, giving praise to the Father for the many blessings He's already bestowed upon us and seeking Him in all that we do. It doesn't mean it's easy; it doesn't mean you won't experience the very real and raw feelings that accompany pregnancy after loss. We are human, and God created each one of us with feelings and emotions. Ultimately, true contentment and satisfaction can only be found in Him. He's beckoning us closer to Him.

Dear Lord, it's a difficult task to be content in all things. It's especially hard when I am faced with a vast array of emotions and feelings surrounding this pregnancy and my loss experience of the past. Help me, Lord, to seek and find true contentment in You. I want to know You more and grow in godliness to be more like Your Son Jesus. It's in His name I pray. Amen.

pen the promise —————————————————————

What are some meaningful steps that you can take today to grow in godliness? Write your ideas in your journal.

Rest Content

pregnancy promise ————————————————————

Reverence brings rest.
The fear of the LORD leads to life; then one rests content, untouched by trouble.

PROVERBS 19:23

Reverence for God brings great peace and rest to our souls. Many verses throughout Scripture discuss the fear of the Lord and benefits that such reverence brings. In this key verse, fear of the Lord not only leads to life, but also to contentment. I love the word picture that this represents because it's so true to think about rest and contentment going hand in hand.

I recall my pregnancy-after-loss days and wish I could say that they were filled with restful contentment as I placed my trust in the Lord. A more accurate depiction would be many days of worry, turmoil, and overloaded busyness just to keep my mind occupied. I wonder, now, how different my days might have been if I had made an intentional, deliberate effort to show reverence to God. In all honesty, my fear distanced me from Him, and I had a hard time taking my cares to the Lord at times.

If you want to rest content today—and I imagine you do, sweet friend—the prescription is found in God's Word. Trust God with your cares, your worries, your joys, and your sorrows. In Matthew 11:28 Jesus said, "Come to me, all you who are weary and burdened, and I will give you rest." From the words of the psalmist to the words of Christ Himself, this message of rest rings true for me, for you, and for all who long to revere the Lord and find contentment in Him.

Dear God, You are worthy of all of our praise. Help me to always revere You as Lord of my life. When I am weary and burdened, give me the strength and the sense to come to You with my cares. In times of great excitement and joy, help me to realize that I need to come to You, as well. Happiness in this world is fleeting, but true joy and contentment are found in You alone, Jesus. Help me to always remember this and to be seeking to rest contentedly in You all of my days. Amen.

pen the promise ─────────────────────────

Can you think of a time on your journey when you've experienced true rest and contentment in God? Write your reflections in your journal.

8

$\mathscr{T}$he $\mathscr{P}$romise of $\mathscr{H}$ope

peace in the promise ————————————————————

Let us hold unswervingly to the hope we profess, for he who promised is faithful.

HEBREWS 10:23

How do we hold *unswervingly* to the hope we profess when our personal history has taken us to the depths of despair? Given your past experience with pregnancy, you may not be holding on to much hope these days as you brace yourself for the worst. You may be white knuckled clinging to hope. But what is the source of that hope? As we think about the promised hope of God, it's imperative that we make a distinction and consider two different types of hope: the hope of this world and heavenly hope. Both are important, both are real, and both can help you navigate the remainder of the journey that lies before you.

When I asked a group of women about times when they felt hopeful during pregnancy after loss, their responses were typically associated with positive reports from the doctor. This makes sense. Hearing a healthy heartbeat, seeing the baby through ultrasound, and receiving reassurance from the doctor brings peace of mind. Such peace, however, is usually fleeting. We know that everything can change in the blink of an eye. Sheralyn battled these honest thoughts when she said:

> I would hear the heartbeat or see him move and feel hope that maybe he was going to be okay. Then as I would think that, my subconscious would kick in and say, "But you had good ultrasounds last time, too."

I know some women who bought Doppler wands to have at home, therefore having the ability to listen to the heartbeat anytime they wanted. I've talked to some women for whom this was a tremendous blessing. I also know a woman for whom this was her worst nightmare, as she couldn't detect the heartbeat and went to the doctor only to receive confirmation that, in fact, there was no heartbeat. You must decide for yourself whether this is something that would be beneficial.

Kristi shared that she had "many moments of hope, almost all of them connected with a positive report from the doctor." Another mother, Holly, agreed with Kristi and went on to say, "Each kick and movement brought peace and hope." We live in an age where we have the technological ability to see and hear our baby in the womb. This is an amazing blessing, not only for the attachment and bonding between the parents and the child within, but also for medical reasons. But no amount of medical technology will bring the supernatural, divine hope that Jesus brings.

I'm sure many of you can relate to the vulnerable words of Sheralyn when she recalled, "It was very difficult to feel hopeful." After all, Sheralyn's journey up to this point consisted of ten years of infertility, three miscarriages along the way, and a son Payton who died eight hours after birth due to a terminal prenatal diagnosis. So, hope that this baby would make it seemed elusive. Against all hope, her son Deklan was born alive and healthy and is now eighteen months old.

Expecting with Hope

Jessica echoed this sentiment of hope being difficult: "Honestly, hope was the hardest thing. Especially during a difficult pregnancy with lots of complications and possibilities for bad outcomes." Jessica was pregnant with twin boys who were diagnosed with twin-to-twin-transfusion syndrome (TTTS). She already had two precious babies in heaven. She gave birth to the twins prematurely, after spending weeks on bed rest. "My first real hopeful moment was when they were delivered and I heard them both squeak," she recalled. "They were alive! To hear that squeak was the first time, I thought, we could do this. They could make it. There's hope."

Jessica's twins are now twenty months old (seventeen months corrected), and according to Jessica: "They're doing well considering how they started. Caleb functions as a normal seventeen-month-old while Ezekiel still has a lot of developmental delays. They are both delightful, happy little boys." Against the odds, they survived and are thriving. Jessica must continue to hold on to hope for their health and for all the other areas of life that we as parents hope for regarding our children.

As you hold on to hope for the healthy birth of your little one, consider also how you can hold on to hope in God. In order to hold unswervingly to the hope we profess (Heb. 10:23), we must first grasp an understanding of what the Bible has to say about hope. There are close to two hundred verses in Scripture that either describe hope or express a person's hopes. The following statements will provide a glimpse into the glory of God's hope, offered and made possible through His Son Jesus. I encourage you to take the time and look up the verse references and reflect on what they mean to you:

> I can look to God for hope (Ps. 39:7).
> God is the source of my hope and He provides rest (Ps. 62:5).
> I will always have hope and give praise (Ps. 71:14).
> My hope is in God's Word (Pss. 119:114; 130:5).
> Hope from God sustains me (Ps. 119:116).
> I can hope while I wait (Ps. 130:5; Mic. 7:7).

Hope renews my strength for the journey (Isa. 40:31).

I am secure in hope (Job 11:18; Heb. 6:19).

Despite my grief, I have hope and am not consumed (Lam. 3:19–22).

Watching is a part of waiting, and I can do so with hope (Mic. 7:7).

I am strong in hope (Ps. 31:24).

I am joyful in hope (Rom. 12:12).

My hope is in the living God, my Savior (1 Tim. 4:10).

My hope anchors my soul (Heb. 6:19).

My hope is confident by faith (Heb. 11:1).

As you read through these statements, are you able to identify with them or do they seem to be elusive? In other words, how do these statements line up with what you would say about yourself during this time of pregnancy after loss?

My hope for you is that these statements are absolute truths in your life. But I realize that may not necessarily be the case. Perhaps you read through this list and are thinking, "Yeah, yeah, yeah . . . I *know* all this." That's wonderful, because just after fearing the Lord—as in revering His holiness—comes knowledge. Proverbs 9:10 says, "The fear of the LORD is the beginning of wisdom, and knowledge of the Holy One is understanding." May understanding be your goal as you fear the Lord, gain wisdom, and get to know Jesus better. As you know Him better, then you begin to more fully understand this heavenly hope. In prayer for you, I echo Paul's words from his letter to the Ephesians:

I keep asking that the God of our Lord Jesus Christ, the glorious Father, may give you the Spirit of wisdom and revelation, so that you may know him better. I pray that the eyes of your heart may be enlightened in order that you may know the hope to which he has called you, the riches of his glorious inheritance in his holy people, and his incomparably great power for us who believe. That power is the same as the mighty strength he exerted when he raised Christ from the dead and seated him at his right hand in the heavenly realms. (Eph. 1:17–20)

Our God is mighty and powerful! He had the power to raise His own Son from the dead so that we may have a life filled with hope. May the power that propels such hope be your lifeline each and every day.

peace in the promise ————————————————

Guide me in your truth and teach me, for you are God my Savior, and my hope is in you all day long.

PSALM 25:5

Hoping . . . All Day Long

I remember well the days of my pregnancies after Chloe died. I was hypersensitive to every flutter, every movement, every ache and symptom or lack thereof. I was hoping upon hope that all would end well, which in my mind (and I think you would agree) meant a healthy baby born alive who stayed alive. I imagine this is your hope for the precious baby you are carrying in pregnancy now. While we hope for the best, we tend to instinctively be preparing for the worst, as though it's a defense mechanism.

Sheralyn admitted going into her appointments and questioning, "Is this the end? Will there be a heartbeat? What will I do if the baby has died?" She's not alone in her questions. Patricia shared the fear she experienced leading up to prenatal visits: "I was so anxious before every prenatal appointment that I would be in tears. I was so afraid that I would find out that a heartbeat could not be found. I did not think I could handle another loss." It makes sense. We want to protect ourselves from the possibility of such hurt again, when in reality this is simply not possible. There's absolutely nothing we can do to prevent our hearts from hurting if loss is to happen again. I've experienced three losses. While each experience was different, the pain that I felt in the aftermath of loss was the same. I grieved deeply because I loved much. There was absolutely nothing I could do to keep myself from loving the child who grew within, whether it was one of my two children who lived, or one of my precious three babies in heaven.

A familiar passage of Scripture about love has much to teach us about hope as well. First Corinthians 13:6–7 declares, "Love does not delight in evil but rejoices with the truth. It always protects, always trusts, always hopes, always perseveres." I wouldn't be surprised if this was a portion of the text you had read during your wedding ceremony. I did. It's from the ever popular "love" chapter. Consequently, it's easy to assume that this passage is geared specifically toward spouses, but in all actuality, it's written so the Christian can know how to best love others. Sure, this may include your spouse, but it covers anyone else, too. Because the passage is primarily about love, we can easily gloss over the fact that it tells us that "love always hopes." As I was pondering this short, yet profound phrase, I got to thinking about you. I was thinking about all the hard work you are doing to brace yourself for the worst-possible scenario and how draining that can be, emotionally and physically. I want to challenge you now, sweet friend. You may continue to deny it, but we both already know that you love your baby within. So remember that *love always hopes.* Love doesn't live in denial and prepare for the worst. Love hopes, believes, and perseveres. May you be encouraged by Paul's words to the Romans when he said:

> For in this hope we were saved. But hope that is seen is no hope at all. Who hopes for what they already have? But if we hope for what we do not yet have, we wait for it patiently. (Rom. 8:24–25)

Expecting with Hope

It's okay to hope—to love—what you cannot see. This is a mark of your faith. You wait patiently for this blessed baby's arrival, and you wait with great hope and expectation. And even as you hope and wait for this little one, may you continually place your hope above.

We tend to fixate our hope on the thing that we desperately desire: a healthy, living baby. There's nothing inherently *wrong* in doing so. As you hope for the life that grows within, may you also be overflowing with hope in the sacrifice of life that brings new life. What if you followed the footsteps of the psalmist in our peace-in-the-promise verse above, and hoped all day long in God your Savior? What if the definition of your hope changed from the sole desire for what you want to simultaneously encompass a core belief in who Jesus is and the peace He promises, regardless of this pregnancy's outcome? That's real hope. That's hope that overflows by the power of the Holy Spirit and ushers in a new perspective for us to truly cling to. Then we can hold unswervingly by faith, boasting only in the glory of God, who is our hope.

peace in the promise ————————————————

Therefore, since we have been justified through faith, we have peace with God through our Lord Jesus Christ, through whom we have gained access by faith into this grace in which we now stand. And we boast in the hope of the glory of God.

ROMANS 5:1–2

Boasting in Hope

It seems strange to boast in hope when it's difficult to maintain any semblance of hope. Boasting in hope means that we know who we are in Christ, our precious Prince of Peace. It means that we can claim hope with confidence because Jesus is our hope. We've traversed some rugged terrain throughout the pages of this book, including fear, contentment, provision, and strength. Countless Scriptures have pointed us back to our Prince of Peace, Jesus. We've been called to rejoice in our sufferings (Rom. 5:3–5; James 1:2), to cast our burdens on the Lord (1 Peter 5:7), and stand firm in faith equipped with the armor of God (Eph. 6:10–17). Even when things don't go as we hope, we can still choose to rejoice and hold on to hope not *because* of our circumstances, but *in spite* of them. This is the hope that we are called to boast about. Sure, many of you—and I pray it is *all* of you—will give birth to a healthy child and will certainly rejoice and celebrate this wonderful life event as it unfolds. We must be prepared, however, to boast in hope even when things don't go in the direction of our heart's deepest desire. Resolve now to stand firm, boasting in hope no matter the outcome. That's precisely what my sweet friend, Mindy, did.

About a year after miscarrying at eight weeks along, Mindy became pregnant again and found great hope in the story of Hannah from the Bible. When asked about hope, Mindy shared these insights:

> Hannah struggled and tried for years to get pregnant. She prayed and made a vow to the Lord that if He remembered her and gave her a son, she would give him back to the Lord all the days of his life. After Samuel was born and weaned, she took him back to the house of the Lord and said, "I prayed for this child, and the LORD has granted me what I asked of him. So now I give him to the LORD. For his whole life he will be given over to the LORD" (1 Sam. 1:27–28). Shortly after we got pregnant, I chose these verses to concentrate on and memorize and remember any time I got anxious or needed hope. I told God, "You have given me this child, and I will give him/her back to You. Even if it is before I am ready to do so." No matter the outcome of my pregnancy, this child was God's, and knowing that made it a little easier to find hope during my pregnancy.

Quite fittingly, when Mindy's son was born alive and well, she and her husband named him Samuel.

Expecting with Hope

Like Mindy, Kristi understood that her hope had to be in God, not in a hoped-for outcome of a living, healthy child. Kristi explained:

> My hope in God's goodness wasn't anything in me, but that was something He brought me through in my journey of loss. But I got irritated that people would see my lack of hope that my baby would be born alive (because that just wasn't promised in Scripture) and think that I wasn't trusting God. I would try to explain—I trust God, but that doesn't mean I know what will happen with my baby—but I felt like a lot of people didn't get that.

Kristi's testimony helps us to remember the true source of our hope. We can boast in the hope of God and His many great and precious promises—for hope and a future, His fearless love, His presence, the truth that He is our sovereign refuge, His provision, His strength, and contentment in Him. There's absolutely nothing wrong with hoping for a healthy, living baby as you continue to journey through this pregnancy. This is a given! Of course you desire nothing more than for your baby to live. But like Mindy and Kristi, we have to be willing to boast in the hope of Christ, no matter what the outcome.

My Pregnancy Prayer for You

God of all hope, I pray that You would be our ultimate source of hope today. Lord, be with this woman now, as she may be afraid to hope because her hopes have been dashed in the past. Help her to keep her hopes in perspective, Lord, as she considers what are valid earthly hopes alongside true and genuine hope in You. There are many ups and downs on this journey, but I pray that You would be constant and faithful through it all. Jesus, You are the living hope. I pray that she would hope in You, regardless of the circumstances that she finds herself in. Amen.

Anchor for My Soul

pregnancy promise —————————————

Hope in God anchors your soul.
We have this hope as an anchor for the soul, firm and secure.

HEBREWS 6:19

"I saw God as my anchor, the one who had everything in His hands and was working according to His plan." These were the faith-filled words of my friend Kristi as she recalled her experience with pregnancy after loss. Yet she admitted that it was sometimes hard to trust in His plan, because none of us can be sure what it is in the end. She's right. We simply do not know. But hope keeps our eyes focused on our faith in God, no matter the circumstances.

Sarah, my sweet friend who continually prayed, *keep knitting, Lord,* during her pregnancy after miscarriage described Jesus as "the hope." She rested in the fact that her son within was actually from God Himself. This brought her comfort and helped to anchor her soul to Jesus.

The hope that Jesus brings is "firm and secure" according to this key verse. Even when your circumstances feel the complete opposite, you can be assured that Jesus can and will anchor your soul. First, you have to give it to Him. He died on the cross so that you and I could have everlasting life. This is our hope. This is the anchor for our hurting, human, heartbroken, yet hopeful souls. Hold on tight, dear friend, and trust that He will never let you go.

Dear Lord, You are our hope. Help me to trust in You with all that I am. You are the anchor for my hurting soul. When life is crazy and things seem to be unraveling and totally out of my control, I can trust that You hold all things together by the power of Your mighty hand. Thank You, Jesus, for being my hope. Amen.

pen the promise ———————————————

Do you feel as though hope anchors your soul? Write your reflections in your journal.

Believing in Hope

pregnancy promise ————————————————

Hope doesn't disappoint.

And we boast in the hope of the glory of God. Not only so, but we also glory in our sufferings, because we know that suffering produces perseverance; perseverance, character; and character, hope. And hope does not put us to shame, because God's love has been poured out into our hearts through the Holy Spirit, who has been given to us.

ROMANS 5:2–5

Betsy and her husband were surprised at the news that they were expecting again. They had a preschool-aged son, but in the year preceding Betsy's pregnancy with Layla, she had experienced the loss of two babies to miscarriages. Layla is now almost a year old, but Betsy looked back on that time with these words:

> God was my ultimate planner. For reasons I will never know, the two babies I lost were not meant to be on this earth. I wouldn't have Layla if I had had either of those babies. Layla was my beautiful little surprise that only He had planned. I put my thoughts and hopes in the fact that He had something special in store for her life, and I couldn't wait to see what that was.

Betsy is boasting in hope, despite the pain of her past. She believes in God's mighty plan, realizing that it often looks different than our own plans, and she has hope for the beautiful life that is in store for her little girl.

As our key verses state so truthfully, it is often our sufferings that bring us to a place of perseverance, character, and hope. As I listened to Betsy share her journey, I couldn't help but think that this is precisely what God has done in her life, through the precious lives of her little ones. It hasn't been easy, but one day it will all be worth it, because hope never disappoints.

Dear Lord, may we always boast in the hope that You provide. I've experienced many sufferings along the way, Lord, and I just ask that You would help me to continue to persevere, that You would develop my character and grow me to be more in love with You, and that I would hold on to the hope of Jesus today and in the days ahead. I want only to boast in You. Amen.

pen the promise ———————————————————

Meditate on the key verses above and write a reflection in your journal on suffering, perseverance, and hope.

God of Hope

pregnancy promise ————————————————

The God of hope brings joy and peace.

May the God of hope fill you with all joy and peace as you trust in him, so that you may overflow with hope by the power of the Holy Spirit.

ROMANS 15:13

I once heard a speaker who simply overflowed with hope, true biblical hope in God. It was a beautiful experience to hear her speak, because God's Holy Word just flowed right out of her. Though she was small and her voice was gentle, the words she spoke were powerful. It was evident that her heart was filled with Jesus and the words she spoke were simply an overflow of that reality in her life. Her joy for Him was real, authentic, and—to be honest—rare.

I saw Jesus shine through this woman, by the power of the Holy Spirit. I wondered what people saw shining through me. I ask you the same question: what do people see shining through you? I'm not suggesting that we try to mimic the character or personality of fellow sinners. But when we see real, authentic joy in Jesus exuding from someone else, that ought to motivate us to get to know Him more.

My pregnancy-after-loss days were some of the hardest. Hope was distant, and I certainly wasn't exuding any semblance of hope. Most days, I was simply trying to make it through without having an emotional meltdown. Maybe that's where you find yourself today. The encouragement lies in our key verse. The God of hope—the God I saw shining through this lovely speaker—is the same God whom we can know and trust today. As we do, the powerful Holy Spirit will bring joy and peace to our restless souls so we, too, will overflow with hope.

People will look on and see Jesus shining through. That's a beautiful thing.

Dear God of hope, I need You. Help me to trust in You fully, Lord. I ask that You bring Your joy and peace into the crevices of my heart that are consumed with the worries of this world. Lord, I want to have a true and authentic faith that exudes joy and the hope You bring. Help me to shine for You, Lord Jesus! Amen.

pen the promise ———————————————————

In your interactions with others, who or what do people see shining through?

Take Heart

pregnancy promise ————————————————

Take heart and hope in the Lord.

Be strong and take heart, all you who hope in the LORD.

PSALM 31:24

Holly admitted honestly how difficult her pregnancy with her daughter was after having experienced four losses. She said:

This was by far the hardest pregnancy. I never bonded with my baby while I was pregnant. Other than my growing tummy, I just went on with life as normal. It was like I was trying to protect my heart. I cried at ultrasounds and worked on changing the nursery from blue to pink. I was finally having my little girl, and I didn't even feel excited. It was weird. I was pretty scared. I knew that God was in control, and I was fine with whatever outcome we experienced. However fear and faith can come hand in hand. I did not have a fear that controlled me, but I did have a fear that came with experience. My baby girl was put into my arms in August of 2013. After feeling a bit like it was too good to be true, I began to bond with my precious miracle. For me, pregnancy after loss was almost harder than the loss itself.

Take heart in knowing that you are not alone, friend. Your story or experience may not look exactly like Holly's, but I imagine you can relate to some aspects of what she shared.

When what you are going through is hard, let your hope in the Lord lead you to a place of peace as you take heart in Him. Jesus tells us to "take heart" when we face trials in this life, because He has overcome the world (John 16:33). This is where our faith and hope are found: in Jesus' overcoming. We have great reason to hope and take heart in Him.

Heavenly Father, thank You for showing me that I am not alone in my experience. It's been a hard road that I sometimes feel as though others don't understand. Thank You, Jesus, for overcoming so that I can take heart and place my hope and trust in You. You are worthy of my praise, Lord, and I give it all to You. You are my hope and my source of all strength to continue to run this race. It's in Your precious name I pray. Amen.

pen the promise

What is your reaction to Holly's story? Write your reflections in your journal.

Always Have Hope

pregnancy promise ————————————————————

God's hope is praiseworthy.

As for me, I will always have hope; I will praise you more and more.

PSALM 71:14

During Kristi's pregnancy, she clung to hope in the goodness of God, knowing full well that there was no guarantee that her baby would be born alive and well. Kristi explains that such hope wasn't anything of or within herself, but was something that God had revealed to her and instilled in her during her journey through loss. As I've said before, there's absolutely nothing *good* about the death of a baby, but God is good even when babies die. This is the hope that Kristi embraced through her loss experience and held onto as she anticipated the arrival of her unborn child.

Such hope is worthy of our praise. In our key verse, the psalmist proclaimed that he would always have hope and continually praise God more and more. If we were to read the entire psalm, we would see that he makes this claim after declaring that God is his rock and his refuge. He trusts in Him completely. It's impossible to have hope in God like Kristi and the psalmist do if we don't fully trust Him. Kristi was able to share her hope with the members of her church while she awaited her little one's arrival. This simple act of faith and obedience causes me to think of the psalmist's very next words: "My mouth will tell of your righteous deeds, of your saving acts all day long—though I know not how to relate them all" (Ps. 71:15). Kristi didn't know what tomorrow would bring, but she was committed to telling others about the saving hope of God, most worthy of praise, despite the uncertainty. Like Kristi, may you always have hope.

Dear God, You are our God of hope. I cannot fathom the extent of Your goodness, even when my circumstances may not seem good at all. Help me, Lord, to trust in You and to have hope in You, always. I desire to have hope in You alone. Give me peace as I place my hope in You, even when things are uncertain. Give me the strength and words to praise You in word and in deed. Amen!

pen the promise —————————————————————

How has God worked through your loss experience(s) to bring you hope? Write about this in your journal.

The Promise of Victory

If this were a neat and tidy world, then I would just start this chapter by stating something ridiculous like, "Congratulations! You have now successfully resolved all outstanding grief from your previous loss. You are now free to give birth to a healthy child without an ounce of fear, anxiety, worry, or trepidation. Sweet victory!"

Well, this isn't a neat and tidy world, and though we've spent a whole lot of time and energy throughout the course of this book working through grief and joy and the crazy imbalance of the two (exacerbated by ever-loving pregnancy hormones), I refuse to place this promise of victory into some sort of triumphant, compartmentalized box. The promise of victory, rather, is truly more of a process, a way of living amidst the mess of whatever situation you find yourself—in this case, wrestling with the many conflicting emotions that rise to the surface when experiencing pregnancy after loss. While you will never "get over" your previous loss(es)—nor would I suggest that you try—you *can* live victoriously today with a healthy balance of grief and joy as you anticipate the birth of a new baby. That doesn't mean that the journey is easy. You will need to gear up for battle as you navigate the mixed bag of grief, joy, and everything in between. With God's help, and His armor, you can have victory today!

peace in the promise —————————————

Finally, be strong in the Lord and in his mighty power. Put on the full armor of God, so that you can take your stand against the devil's schemes.

EPHESIANS 6:10–11

Get Dressed, Girlfriend!

No, I'm not talking about your physical wardrobe. Though it's always fun to add a new pair of shoes or stylish handbag to the mix. But I digress; these are accessories. Let's talk essentials.

In Ephesians 6, we are commanded to put on the full armor of God. We are not dressing for some dainty dinner party, ladies. We are gearing up for full-on battle. That's the call of any Christian, as we must be prepared for the enemy's schemes. The full armor of God is reserved for those who have surrendered their lives to Christ, who *know* the Prince of Peace. So I ask, do you know the Prince of Peace (appendix A)? Knowing Jesus does not and will not win you a get-out-of-trials-free card. From a human perspective, one might think it would be fabulous to be able to just skip over particularly painful periods in life. But it's in walking through the tough stuff, with eyes fixed on eternity, that we grow to be more like Christ. James 1:2–4 tells us:

Consider it pure joy, my brothers and sisters, whenever you face trials of many kinds, because you know that the testing of your faith produces perseverance. Let perseverance finish its work so that you may be mature and complete, not lacking anything.

If we are going to grow and mature in Christ, we need to be geared up and ready for battle. This journey of grief we've traversed, followed by subsequent pregnancy, has the propensity to grow us in His likeness or crumble us to pieces. Peter sent us a similar message when he wrote:

Dear friends, do not be surprised at the fiery ordeal that has come on you to test you, as though something strange were happening to you. But rejoice inasmuch as you participate in the sufferings of Christ, so that you may be overjoyed when his glory is revealed. (1 Peter 4:12–13)

We ought not be surprised by trials. Sure, our journey is unique, but we will all face struggles. We shouldn't be surprised, because our Sovereign God is not surprised. He prepares us for battle by telling us exactly what armor we will need.

The full armor of God consists of the belt of truth, the breastplate of righteousness, feet fitted with readiness that comes from the gospel of peace, the shield of faith, the helmet of salvation, and the sword of the Spirit, which is the Word of God (Eph. 6:10–17). Let's take a deeper look at each piece.

Belt of Truth
Buckle your belt of truth, sweet friend. Sure, it may be maternity size these days, but a necessary piece of armor, nonetheless. The believer's belt of truth means that as followers of Jesus, you are committed to truth; both the truths of God found in His Word, as well as an overall attitude of truthfulness. Let's consider the implications of these two aspects of truth in relation to the experience of pregnancy after loss.

Being committed to Truth—with a capital T—means on the most basic level that we do precisely as James instructed when he wrote, "Do not merely listen to the word, and so deceive yourselves. Do what it says" (James 1:22). You can't get much clearer than that. In order to "do what it says," we need to know what it says. Read it, listen to it, memorize it, and write it on the tablet of your heart (Prov. 7:3). Seek knowledge, wisdom, and understanding from the Word so that you may know and live by and for the Truth. May each of us be able to echo the words of the psalmist when he wrote, "I have hidden your word in my heart that I might not sin against you" (Ps. 119:11). Consider the words of Jesus when He said, "If you hold to my teaching, you are really my disciples. Then you will know the truth, and the truth will set you free" (John 8:31–32). Throughout this book, you've delved into truth from God's Word. I paraphrase James when I say, Don't just read it . . . do it! Stand firm with your belt of truth fastened tightly and trust that you are secure in living out God's truths.

A part of living in light of truth means possessing an overall attitude of truthfulness. The greatest way you can apply this as you journey through pregnancy after loss is to ask yourself, "What is true?" Parking yourself amidst irrational fears, worst-case scenarios, and what-ifs will only lead you to succumb to that which is not true. Yes, there are milestones to look forward to and overcome, and there are appointments that bring a sense of peace, but throughout, it is important to focus on what is true. Your baby is alive. Your baby is growing within. You are ___ weeks along and have ___ weeks left to birth, Lord willing. I encourage you to speak these very basic, factual truths aloud when irrational untruth creeps in and leads you down a path of fear and worry. The facts of your situation, secondary to God's truth, will guard your heart and bring peace in those moments of worry.

Breastplate of Righteousness

The breastplate of righteousness refers to the truth that Christ's righteousness blankets those of us who've placed our trust in Him.

In Paul's second letter to the Corinthians, he wrote, "God made him who had no sin to be sin for us, so that in him we might become the righteousness of God" (2 Cor. 5:21). The one "who had no sin" is Jesus. He took our place and paid the penalty for our sin. So as we place our trust in Him, God looks upon us and, instead of seeing our sinfulness, He sees Christ's righteousness. Having been declared righteous because of Christ, we are called to live holy and obedient lives. First Peter 1:14–16 says,

> As obedient children, do not conform to the evil desires you had when you lived in ignorance. But just as he who called you is holy, so be holy in all you do; for it is written: "Be holy, because I am holy."

Holiness and obedience to God must be evident in our day-to-day lives. If we claim to live for God, then we need to examine some important areas of our lives as we journey through this experience of pregnancy after loss—areas like anxiety, fear, and contentment.

We've discussed these issues at length throughout this book already. If we are gearing up with the breastplate of righteousness, we need to remember that Christ took our place. It is His righteousness that covers us. Thus, if we journey through this pregnancy with an attitude of discontentment or are consumed by worry and fear, we are, in a sense, living as though Jesus is not enough. Yet, He bore the greatest burden—our sinfulness—so that we might wear His righteousness and look to Him to daily bear our burdens. There will be temptations and "scares" along the way, as you walk in day-by-day anticipation of the birth of your baby. Remember this truth:

> No temptation has overtaken you except what is common to mankind. And God is faithful; he will not let you be tempted beyond what you can bear. But when you are tempted, he will also provide a way out so that you can endure it. (1 Cor. 10:13)

God is faithful. He will give you strength to endure as you fix your heart and mind on Him.

Feet Fitted with Readiness

Swollen as they may be, get those feet ready! I invite you now to put on your faith shoes and walk confidently, one step at a time, in the path the Lord has prepared for you. I know this road has been long and hard. There's no assurance that it's going to get easier. The season of grief that you've weathered—continue to weather—has been difficult. This time of pregnancy after loss has brought with it new challenges as you try to strike a balance between grief and joy and everything in between. When your baby is born, there will be a whole new set of struggles to contend with. Such is the nature of life.

If your feet are fitted for readiness, you will be able to walk through the joys and the sorrows with a humble, holy confidence in the Savior, no matter the opposition you face. Having feet fitted for readiness means that you are on guard, alert, and aware of the Devil's schemes and his eagerness to plant seeds of doubt and lies in your mind. Admit it, now is a vulnerable time—a time where emotions are running high and faith can seem hard to grasp. You must be alert, but do not be paralyzed!

You have a story, sweet friend. We all do. I believe the Lord is still writing our stories, but let us testify all along the way of His mercy, His goodness, and His unfailing love toward us. Romans 10:15 reminds us of a verse from the Old Testament prophet Isaiah, when it says, "And how can anyone preach unless they are sent? As it is written: 'How beautiful are the feet of those who bring good news.'" Let us bring good news simply by how we live and walk in the faith of our Father, who continues to pen the progress.

Shield of Faith

Just to be clear, let's first identify what your shield of faith is *not*. It's not your husband (as godly as he may be), it's not your pastor or some other spiritual leader in your life. It's not your church, your fellow Christian friends, or any religion you follow. Too often, these people and institutions become a crutch to our faith, particularly when the going gets tough. Rather than relying on people and practices, we must rely on the relationship we have with Christ. As such, our shield of faith is our faith in God. The object of our faith is Jesus Christ.

Ephesians 6:16 calls us to "take up the shield of faith, with which you can extinguish all the flaming arrows of the evil one." Our faith protects us from the Devil's schemes. By our faith, we can stand firm and walk courageously through the trials of life. This is our shield. As we recall the promise of God as our Sovereign Refuge (chapter 4), we are reminded of numerous verses that tell us that God Himself is our shield! If you are going to cower during this pregnancy, cower only under the safe and sovereign refuge of your shield of faith. There lies true protection. Activate your shield in prayer. Talk to God; pour out your heart to Him. When you are nervous about an appointment or concerned as the milestones pass by, pray to Him and ask Him to be your shield of faith in that moment.

Helmet of Salvation

Any soldier in their right mind wouldn't dare enter battle without a helmet. The same is true for the spiritual battle that we Christians face in day-to-day living on the battleground of this fallen world. We must not forget our salvation, ladies. Too often, we get so wrapped up in the busyness of life, the craziness of schedules, and the headaches of our circumstances, that we fail to remember that we were bought with a price—a steep price, at that. May these words of the psalmist be the prayer of your heart: "Restore to me the joy of your salvation and grant me a willing spirit, to sustain me" (Ps. 51:12). Be willing to walk the path that God has prepared for you, my friend. Don't bow in surrender to anyone or anything unless it's Jesus!

Remembering the joy of our salvation helps us to fix our eyes on what is eternal, rather than what's temporal. James 4:14–15 says,

Why, you do not even know what will happen tomorrow. What is your life? You are a mist that appears for a little while and then vanishes. Instead, you ought to say, "If it is the Lord's will, we will live and do this or that."

Rather than being so fixated on what will (or will not) happen, we need to remember that we are secure in our salvation because of Christ. We are called to draw near to God with a heart that has full assurance of faith (Heb. 10:22). Our salvation is our hope, made possible because of Jesus, the Prince of Peace. Our earthly lives are temporary, and as we are all keenly aware, we are not promised another day. We also know that this is not the end. We can have great confidence and assurance of our future heavenly home because of the fact that Jesus saves.

Sword of the Spirit

When Paul mentioned this final piece of gear, he referred to it as "the sword of the Spirit, which is the word of God" (Eph. 6:17). He explicitly stated that we are to gear up with the Word. Likened to a sword the Word can be used offensively and defensively in battle. You may recall that in chapter 6, we talked at length about how we gain strength from God's Word. The same idea applies here. God's Word is truly a weapon for us. When Satan tempts us with lies, we can combat with truth. This is exactly the example that Jesus set for us when He was tempted by Satan in the wilderness (Matt. 4:1–11). When you know the Word, it wells up within you by the power of the Holy Spirit to bring comfort and peace and to combat lies precisely when you need it.

It is necessary that we gear up with the *full* armor of God for this very reason: "For our struggle is not against flesh and blood, but against the rulers, against the authorities, against the powers of this dark world and against the spiritual forces of evil in the heavenly realms" (Eph. 6:12). We need to be on guard against the Enemy's schemes. He wants to plant seeds of doubt and blatant lies into our minds. He is the father of lies, and he would like nothing more than to see one of God's girls sink to a place of worry and despair. We need to rise above, stand firm, and wave our banners of victory high for all to see, armed with the gear that God provides.

peace in the promise ————————————————————

May we shout for joy over your victory and lift up our banners in the name of our God. . . . Some trust in chariots and some in horses, but we trust in the name of the LORD our God.

PSALM 20:5, 7

Live Victoriously Today

Don't wait until this baby is born and resting safely in your arms to live victoriously. Stake your claim on victory now! The truth is, there will always be some new challenge, struggle, or trial that attempts to hold you back from living victoriously for Christ. That's the nature of this sinful, fallen world. Remember, Jesus already holds the victory because He overcame the grave. We need to decide if we are going to glory in the resurrection or live in the shadows of our circumstances. Jesus said in John 16:33, "I have told you these things, so that in me you may have peace. In this world you will have trouble. But take heart! I have overcome the world." He wants us to possess peace in this difficult world, made possible by His victorious overcoming. Paul's first letter to the Corinthians celebrates this victory:

When the perishable has been clothed with the imperishable, and the mortal with immortality, then the saying that is written will come true: "Death has been swallowed up in victory." "Where, O death, is your victory? Where, O death, is your sting?" The sting of death is sin, and the power of sin is the law. But thanks be to God! He gives us the victory through our Lord Jesus Christ. (1 Cor. 15:54–57)

Victory reigns because Jesus reigns. Jesus overcame the grave so that we could live life to the full. Because He overcame, so too may we. Our faith in Him helps us to overcome, and we claim the victory when we are able to keep His commands. The greatest command is to love God. The second is to love others. In the gospel of Mark, Jesus is asked which of all the commandments was the most important. Jesus replied:

"'Love the Lord your God with all your heart and with all your soul and with all your mind and with all your strength.' The second is this: 'Love your neighbor as yourself.' There is no commandment greater than these." (Mark 12:30–31)

Loving your neighbor simply means loving others, including the unborn baby whom you carry within—the one whom some of you are desperately trying *not* to love. Embrace this child, this gift. Claim victory over Satan's lies and take these words to heart, sweet friend. You are called to love God and love others. You love because He loved you first (1 John 4:19).

My Pregnancy Prayer for You

Jesus, You alone hold the victory! Help us to remember that when we are weary from the battle that rages in our heads and in our hearts. I pray, Lord, that You would give the woman reading these words a supernatural strength to live victoriously in You. May she, like the Proverbs 31 woman, be able to laugh at the days to come because she stands firm in faith. Be with her now, Lord, as she makes the choice to live victoriously today, which is only possible because You overcame. In your precious name we pray. Amen.

Expecting with Hope

The Day I Overcame

pregnancy promise ————————————————————

Because you belong to God, the victory is already yours.
You, dear children, are from God and have overcome them, because the
one who is in you is greater than the one who is in the world.

1 JOHN 4:4

I remember quite vividly the day I overcame. Fear had taken up residence in my heart as we counted the days, marking off week by week on the calendar, until our sweet baby would arrive *safely* in our arms. Having received a terminal diagnosis at twenty-weeks with our first daughter, Chloe, I was so incredibly nervous about having that routine ultrasound with this baby.

In the days leading up to the ultrasound, my husband and I disagreed about whether or not to find out the gender of our baby. We hadn't learned the gender of our first child until we heard the news, "It's a boy!" in the delivery room. We had been ecstatic. We hadn't intended to find out gender for Chloe, but once we knew that her time on earth would be limited, we'd decided it was best to know so that we could get to know her. With our third child, my husband wanted very much to be surprised and to experience joy and excitement like we had with our oldest. I, on the other hand, *needed* to know. Not because I couldn't exercise patience or wanted to plan a nursery. I needed to know so that I could begin allowing myself to bond with my baby.

When I opened up to my husband, he understood and agreed. So we entered that twenty-week ultrasound with fear and anticipation and learned that we were having a little girl. Within a day or two, I made my way to the local craft and home-décor store to find the perfect thing for our precious girl. It couldn't be pink—that was Chloe's color. My eyes were drawn to a beautiful framed piece of wall art. A white frame and matte surrounded an inlet that housed a cross, comprised of lavender and lime-green clothing buttons that embellished a matching patterned paper background. Yes, this was it. The day I overcame . . .

I had let fear rule for too long and operated under the illusion that I could somehow keep myself from bonding with the baby who grew within. When I saw the cross decoration that would be the centerpiece of her nursery (and still adorns her wall, one move and five years later), I was reminded of the One who endured the cross and truly overcame. Jesus conquered sin and death on that cross, making a way for each of us to have eternal life in heaven. While I still grieve Chloe, I can grieve with hope. I realized in that moment, in the middle of the craft store, that I was free to enjoy the remainder of my pregnancy. Not because of anything about me, but because of Christ in me who had already set me free.

Heavenly Father, may today be a day of overcoming for me. Set me free by the power of the cross of Your Son Jesus Christ. Instill in me a conquering spirit as I battle to claim joy during my pregnancy. Give me Your grace, Lord, as I continue to wrestle with the grief and hold on to hope for my baby who now grows within. You are greater than any worldly trial, Lord. Help me to trust in You. Amen.

pen the promise ─────────────────────────

Reflect on your current pregnancy and make a list of any/all small victories you've achieved and celebrate them. If you can't think of anything for your list, write down one or two things that you could do this week that you would consider a victory.

Expecting with Hope

Be Still

pregnancy promise ————————————————

The Lord will fight for you.
"The LORD will fight for you; you need only to be still."

EXODUS 14:14

If you've experienced pregnancy far enough along to be able to feel the kicks and flutters of your little one growing within, then you know the reassurance that those movements can bring. Sometimes, the kicks feel more like a full out ninja ambush from inside and take you by complete surprise. Other times, a lack of movement may cause feelings of uneasiness or worry, causing you to stop, rest, and wait for the kicks to resume.

You've probably received instruction from your nurse or obstetrician to make a routine of counting the kicks daily, particularly once the third trimester of pregnancy sets in. For those of us who've been impacted by loss in the past, it doesn't take a whole lot of coaxing or fancy educational materials to convince us of the importance of this daily routine, the goal of which is to help reduce preventable stillbirths. This habit more than likely comes naturally as we continually seek out reassurance of our baby's well-being, especially because of a history of loss. Just as we still ourselves to monitor the movements of our babies during pregnancy, it's important that we still our souls to monitor the work of God in our lives.

Just as you've made it a routine to monitor the movement of your baby who continues to grow within, make it a point to monitor the movement of God in and through your life. Take time to be still before God, trusting that, as it says in today's verse, He is fighting for us. Our instructions? Be still. Be still before Him today, and tomorrow, and then the next day, and so on. When we still ourselves before the Lord, we are able to see the wonderful work He is doing on our behalf.

Dear God, give me the wisdom to know the importance of being still before You. Help me to be attuned to the work You have done, are doing, and will continue to do in my life and in the life of my child. Give me rest as I quiet myself before You, and reveal to me the many ways in which You are fighting for me. Thank You, Lord, for fighting for me, Your child. Amen.

pen the promise ───────────────────────────

Set aside at least ten minutes today to be still before the Lord, attuned to His presence in your life. During this time, pray, sing a favorite worship song, or simply read over today's key verse and listen. Journal about your experience.

Gear Up

pregnancy promise ——————————————————

God provides all we need to stand firm in faith.

Finally, be strong in the Lord and in his mighty power. Put on the full armor of God, so that you can take your stand against the devil's schemes.

EPHESIANS 6:10–11

After LeeAnn experienced the loss of her son, Eli, at sixteen weeks along in January 2013, she got her own feet as well as her next baby's feet fitted for readiness. Confident that she would be pregnant again and birth a healthy child, she bought a pair of what she calls "faith socks" for a future baby. She wrote the date on the tag of the socks the day that she bought them—January 30, 2013—and placed them in her jewelry box. LeeAnn explained: "I needed something tangible I could touch to remember this will happen. I will place these sweet socks on my baby after loss." On January 22, 2014, less than a year from the date that she wrote on her baby-to-be's faith socks, LeeAnn gave birth to a healthy little boy. With boldness and faith, she honored Eli with this token of remembrance, but looked forward with hope to how God would answer her heart's desire.

Let me be clear. Nothing in LeeAnn's power, or the socks for that matter, allowed her to become pregnant and birth a healthy child. But what I appreciate about her story is that she had faith to believe that her heart's longing would be fulfilled, and until that time, she chose to do something to honor Eli, yet look forward with hope. What a beautiful balance of grief and celebration of what was to come. LeeAnn stood firm, an example for you and me both.

Heavenly Father, prepare my feet for readiness for whatever this journey may bring. Lord, I pray that You would give me faith to believe that You have my best at heart. Help me to trust in You with all the details surrounding my pregnancy. Help me to live, Lord, as though my baby is going to make it. By Your mighty power, help me to be firm in faith—in times of rejoicing and in times of adversity. In Jesus' name. Amen.

pen the promise

Write your reaction to LeeAnn's story of her "faith socks." What is something tangible that you can do as you look forward with hope to the birth of your baby? Write about it in your journal.

Victory in the Diaper Aisle

pregnancy promise ————————————————————

The ultimate victory is found in Christ.

But thanks be to God! He gives us the victory through our Lord Jesus Christ.

1 CORINTHIANS 15:57

Victory sometimes comes in the most unexpected places. For my friend Sheralyn, it was in the diaper aisle, just a few days before her son Deklan was born. Because of her painful pregnancy past, it was difficult for Sheralyn to do some of the preparations for Deklan's arrival. After all, she had experienced years of infertility, three miscarriages, and then the death of her newborn son, Peyton, just 8 hours after his birth. The thought of birthing a healthy baby to care for on this earth was a wonderfully elusive dream, and thoughts of doom had taken up residence in her heart.

In recalling her moment in the diaper aisle, Sheralyn said: "I stood in front [of] the diaper aisle for ten minutes, looking at them and thinking to myself, 'If only I could bring myself to touch them.' I finally reached for a bag of Huggies and I started crying hard." I consider this a great victory! She realized the need, she formed a thought of what she had to do, and she did it! Yes, the tears came, but that's okay. I imagine you can relate to moments similar to Sheralyn's as you think about your own pregnancy. Hard moments filled with tears for so many reasons: grief over the past, joy over the present, fear for the future blended with excitement and anticipation. It's a mixed bag, that's for sure.

As Sheralyn shared her story with me, I imagined myself standing beside her in the diaper aisle, tears streaming down my own face, cheering her on! As I write these words now, I am doing the same for you—whatever situation you are in, whatever obstacle you see standing in your way, I am cheering for you with arms raised high to Jesus who holds the ultimate victory in the palms of His nail-pierced hands. In Him, you can do all things!

Heavenly Father, You alone hold the victory! Thank You for sending Your Son Jesus to overcome sin and death so that I can overcome the obstacles in my life by relying on Your strength to see me through. I pray, Lord, that You would give me a vision for what lies beyond the many obstacles that I see in my way to true joy. Give me eyes to see through the challenges and to look to You for strength as I rest in the truth that the battle is already won. Help me to live victoriously always. Amen.

pen the promise —————————————————

As you think about your pregnancy, what are the two greatest obstacles you are facing today? Is there a fear to overcome or a task to complete? Write them down and spend some time journaling ideas of how you can face those obstacles.

Expecting with Hope

More Than Conquerors

pregnancy promise ─────────────────────────

God is *for* you and nothing can separate you from His love.
No, in all these things we are more than conquerors through him who
loved us.

ROMANS 8:37

Nichelle is one of those women who is real and genuine, and you can
just tell that she loves Jesus. Not unlike any one of us, she's had a painful journey to motherhood, marred with loss and infertility struggles.
Nichelle shared her thoughts on victory:

> I tried to have victory over His will for me to have another child.
> Somehow, I felt if I willed it enough it would surely be His will
> also. I would win and be victorious! But God's truths were in front
> of me; the victory is not becoming pregnant after my losses, or
> even having a child born alive. The victory is in the salvation that
> my Lord offers through His Son. Victory is that the battle for my
> heart is won. Victory is the price paid for me.

I couldn't agree with Nichelle more. True victory is found in Christ.
His love, displayed so lavishly on the cross, is a bond that cannot be broken.

Each and every one of us are more than conquerors because of
Him. There is nothing we can do, not do, attain, or lose that will
separate us from His love. We overcome because He overcame. Take
heart in this truth today, dear friend, and know that God's good and
perfect will for you is made complete simply by continuing to trust in
the One who overcame.

Heavenly Father, I praise You because absolutely nothing can separate those of us who've trusted in Your Son Jesus from Your love. Thank You for lavishing Your love upon me and for the unbreakable bond of such love. Help me to overcome the feelings of fear, anxiety, worry, or turmoil that I'm experiencing; help me to trust in You. Give me eyes to see with clarity that true victory is found in You and by placing my trust in You. In You, Lord, I know I can overcome any test or trial I endure in this life. Thank You for reigning victorious, Jesus. Amen.

pen the promise ———————————————

Write your reaction to Nichelle's thoughts on victory. Can you relate to her attempts to manipulate God's will? Can you relate to the revelation she describes about victory?

The Promise of Joy

peace in the promise —————————————————

May the God of hope fill you with all joy and peace as you trust in him, so that you may overflow with hope by the power of the Holy Spirit.

ROMANS 15:13

When we started off this journey together through the pages of this book, I wanted you to know from the start that God has a plan and a future for you (and your baby): "to prosper you and not to harm you" (Jer. 29:11). In the darkest valleys and in the most joyful seasons of life, this promise remains constant and true. It may seem cliché, but it is my great hope that you've found truth that sets you free and brings peace. You can reclaim joy despite all that you've lost, because the Prince of Peace brings joy.

Whether you've admitted it to yourself or not, this pregnancy—the miracle of the life that you carry within—is certainly reason to rejoice. You might be mad at me for saying this, but I am overflowing with joy for you. Truly, I am. I also weep over the path that has gotten you here, knowing that you have a child (or children) in heaven. Romans

12:15 asserts, "Rejoice with those who rejoice; mourn with those who mourn." This verse pretty much sums up my heart for you! I rejoice for the baby you carry now, and I mourn for you as you grieve the loss of your baby who is in heaven. Then again, I rejoice, because that baby *is* in heaven due to God's amazing grace displayed by Jesus on the cross: the crux of our hope. It's a confusing time—pregnancy after loss— because people just expect you to be extra joyful over the baby you now carry. They don't understand that it's impossible to "move on," because they clearly have and would certainly be more comfortable if you did, as well. For many women experiencing pregnancy after loss, there's lingering grief, anxiety to the max, and guilt because you aren't as joyful as you *should* be. Other times, the guilt takes over because you are *too* joyful about the pregnancy, and feel as though you are forgetting your baby who died. How do you explain that to the outsider looking in? The truth is, you can't. And you don't have to. Through it all, the Lord promises to be present, your hope, your strength, and more. I pray that this book has helped you to see a glimpse of that; that peace is possible through Jesus. Not only peace, but hope and joy as you *enjoy* this baby that is yet to be born.

Hope in Christ brings joy and peace beyond our ability to comprehend. By possessing a true hope in our trustworthy God, there is an abundance of joy and peace by the power of the Holy Spirit. Just as our peace-in-the-promise verse states, God fills you with joy and peace so that you may overflow with hope. First John 3:1 says, "See what great love the Father has lavished on us, that we should be called children of God! And that is what we are!" It's God's amazing love that brings hope and joy to our lives.

peace in the promise —————————————————

Rejoice always, pray continually, give thanks in all circumstances; for this is God's will for you in Christ Jesus.

1 THESSALONIANS 5:16–18

Expecting with Hope

God's Will for You

As you've walked the painful road of miscarriage or infant loss on your journey to motherhood, perhaps experiencing a series of losses and fertility struggles along the way, it's understandable that you may wonder what exactly is God's will for your life. That's a valid question, worthy of something more than a pat answer. Sometimes the truth is hard. And the truth in this matter is that I don't know exactly how your circumstances will play out. I hold on to great hope for you as you continue your pregnancy with this precious one who grows within. I pray fervently for his or her safe arrival into your arms and for this precious child of yours to grow to love the Lord at the earliest possible age. I pray that this child's life would be one that honors the Prince of Peace and brings glory to His name. Yes, these are my prayers, but that doesn't mean that they are promises in line with God's will for your life.

His Word is filled with promises for your life, and the peace-in-the-promise verses from 1 Thessalonians 5 provide a direct answer to the question of what is God's will for your life and for mine: "Rejoice always, pray continually, [and] give thanks in all circumstances" (vv. 16–18). He doesn't give us the blueprint for what our lives will look like with regard to experiences. But He does give us these three specific instructions for how to handle life experiences and to walk according to His good and perfect will. Ephesians 2:10 does assure us that God has a plan for us: "For we are God's handiwork, created in Christ Jesus to do good works, which God prepared in advance for us to do." With that beautiful promise in mind, let us let go of our need to know *what* we will be doing and focus on *how* we will be doing it.

Rejoice Always

Rejoicing *always* seems a bit impractical, don't you think? I admit I struggle with this, especially when anxiety is a factor. It's hard to rejoice when your heart and mind are racing with anxious thoughts. But this isn't the only time Scripture instructs us to rejoice always. In

Paul's letter to the Philippians, he proclaimed, "Rejoice in the Lord always. I will say it again: Rejoice!" (Phil. 4:4). Notice that Paul said it twice here. It must be really important.

You may be wondering how you can manage to rejoice when you are still working through the grief and balancing out the all-consuming anxiety. Rest in His promises, sweet friend. Remember the truths that we've unpacked throughout the course of this book. Go back to them and dig into the Word for your answers. Practice full obedience to God's Word and His instructions for you. When thoughts and fears run out of control, "take captive every thought to make it obedient to Christ" (2 Cor. 10:5). Find great comfort, as I have, in Psalm 94:19 which says, "When anxiety was great within me, your consolation brought me joy." What a precious reminder that it's not our circumstances that bring us joy. Rather, it's our Savior! Rejoicing always is not a natural response for us in our own strength. But by knowing Christ and having the power of the Holy Spirit within, you are able to rejoice always.

Pray Continually

When you don't feel like rejoicing, go to God in prayer and ask Him to bestow upon you a joyful spirit. If you are concerned about your circumstances, you can still be joyful in the Lord. He wants you to pour out those concerns to Him in prayer. With God, we can live in a state of joy while simultaneously navigating the ups and downs of life. "With God all things are possible" (Matt. 19:26). I can't think of a single person who could say that they haven't experienced a trial or a difficult season in life. We all go through them. As Christians, our hope is that we don't have to go through trials alone and we need not endure hardships in misery.

The experience of pregnancy after loss is confusing because for many it *is* a trial, yet others look on and see it solely as a tremendous blessing. They don't recognize the struggle. Absolutely this baby is a blessing, but that doesn't mean that the process of pregnancy isn't a challenge, particularly when pregnancy has ended in loss before. Ask the Lord to give insight to family and friends who don't understand your caution.

Pregnancy after loss is time of intertwined joy and sorrow. Follow James's instructions when he says, "Is anyone among you in trouble? Let them pray. Is anyone happy? Let them sing songs of praise. . . . The prayer of a righteous person is powerful and effective" (James 5:13,16).

Give Thanks in All Circumstances

Do not be confused; this final command of 1 Thessalonians 5:16–18 is not an instruction to give thanks *for* all circumstances. Rather, it's an instruction to give thanks *in* all circumstances. There's a difference. In all circumstances, as downright hard as they may be—the loss of your baby(ies), the struggle with infertility, and now pregnancy wrought with fear—we are called to give thanks. Because in the smack dab middle of whatever it is you face today, God is there. If you know Jesus, the Holy Spirit is living inside you and gives you the power to see beyond the temporal and into what is eternal. As negative attitudes invade your mind, pause and reframe with gratitude. For example:

Attitude: I'm sure this baby won't make it.
Gratitude: Thank You, Lord, for giving me _____ weeks with this baby already.

Attitude: I'm a failure as a mother. I couldn't carry the last baby. Why should I be allowed to carry this child now?
Gratitude: Thank You, Lord, for choosing me to be the mother to a baby in heaven and to this baby I carry now.

Attitude: If only I can get past this particular milestone, then I will be relieved and more at peace.
Gratitude: Thank You, Jesus, for being my peace even when it's difficult. Help me to rely on You all the way through.

Consider the negative thoughts and attitudes that have been part of your internal dialogue throughout this pregnancy. How can you reframe those attitudes into an expression of gratitude? The circumstances haven't changed, but by reframing those thoughts, your perspective on the circumstances changes. Your existence as a follower of Jesus transcends the pains of this world, because you, my friend, are living with eyes fixed on heaven.

peace in the promise —————————

And let us run with perseverance the race marked out for us.

HEBREWS 12:1

Run the Race with Joy

Perhaps the last thing a pregnant woman wants to hear is anything having to do with running. I'm not even pregnant, and the *thought* of running makes me short of breath and causes me to go searching for my rescue inhaler just as a precaution. What's more, running with joy? Thank goodness I'm not speaking literally, because it's hard for me to believe that anyone can physically run with joy. I know some of you runner-type gals are sitting there shaking your heads in disagreement as you read. Let's just say—in case you hadn't figured it out—I'm not the running type. I am, however, the running-after-Jesus type, and that's precisely what I'm talking about here.

Our peace-in-the-promise verse from Hebrews encourages us to run the race set before us. For you, the current race is your pregnancy. It may seem like a marathon at the moment, but in the race of life, it's more like the warm-up lap. Please know that I don't intend to minimize the experience by any means. I consider it a warm-up lap merely because the parenting of this child will be a major part of the race! Let's look at the larger context of this verse:

Expecting with Hope

Let us throw off everything that hinders and the sin that so easily entangles. And let us run with perseverance the race marked out for us, fixing our eyes on Jesus, the pioneer and perfecter of faith. For the joy set before him he endured the cross, scorning its shame, and sat down at the right hand of the throne of God." (Heb. 12:1–2)

The race isn't about making it through the pregnancy or surviving parenthood. Rather, it's about looking to Jesus through it all, and that, my friend, is the mark of growing as a follower of Christ. We all have lives that are complex and messy at times. We are charged with the task to run the race for the joy set before us, just as Jesus—who *is* our joy—did Himself.

Several other passages give similar encouragement to keep running the race. In Paul's letter to the Philippians, he said, "I press on toward the goal to win the prize for which God has called me heavenward in Christ Jesus" (Phil. 3:14). The prize is growing to know Jesus better. In verses 7–11, Paul gave passionate testimony about his own walk with the Lord. He said that he considered everything a loss compared to the great worth of knowing Jesus in an authentic way (Phil. 3:8). We are called to press on, to know Jesus better, and to keep running the race set before us.

We get more encouragement to continue the race in the book of Hebrews:

We who have run for our very lives to God have every reason to grab the promised hope with both hands and never let go. It's an unbreakable spiritual lifeline, reaching past all appearances right to the very presence of God where Jesus, running on ahead of us, has taken up his permanent post as high priest for us, in the order of Melchizedek. (Heb. 6:18–20 MSG)

Run for your lives to God and grab hold of His promised hope, sweet friend. Jesus runs on ahead of you and has taken up His post as high priest so that we may go directly to God with hearts surrendered to Christ. In the Old Testament, only the high priest had direct access to God. Jesus came to earth, lived a perfect life, died upon the cross, and rose from the dead so that we could have direct access to the Father by trusting in the Son. Jesus—our Prince of Peace—paid the penalty for our sins and has taken up His post as permanent high priest for all eternity. We now have the ability to approach God directly and with confidence as we place our hope in Christ. As you wade through the ups and downs and twists and turns that this pregnancy after loss experience brings, you can do so with joy because you have Jesus as your companion for the journey.

peace in the promise ————————————————

Weeping may last for the night, but a shout of joy comes in the morning.

PSALM 30:5 (NASB)

Tears of Joy

On the morning of June 30, 2008, love flooded my heart in a way I never knew possible. Aiyana Elise Drake entered this world screaming. She was alive and healthy, and I was relieved. As the nurse handed her to me to hold for the first time, I just sobbed hysterically. This was the same nurse who was by my side when Chloe had been born just two years earlier—alive, but gasping for breath and not offering even the hint of one cry her whole life. So to hear Aiyana's cries was overwhelming. I remember the nurse repeating, "It's okay, it's okay. She's fine, she's just fine." I knew she was fine, but in that moment it was as though I could finally let my heart believe it. It's funny as I look back on the experience of Aiyana's birth, because she was crying for quite a long time. It was nothing of concern, but I remember the nurses making remarks about it. I considered it an extra blessing from the Lord to be able to hear her cry. To me, this meant that she really was okay. She really was alive. She really was breathing steadily. Love overwhelmed me. As I tried to process all the emotions and feelings of the experience, I was blown away by the fact that God had graced me with enough love for all of my children.

I wasn't alone in this reaction. My friend Kristi said that when her son Caleb was born, she kept saying "He's alive. . . . Thank You, God!" repeatedly, and even has it on video. Whether you verbalize it, cry through it, or stay calm, cool, and collected, I imagine your heart's cry will be similar when you can see, touch, and hold your healthy, living baby for the first time. Your child's birth experience will be a picture of our peace-in-the-promise verse, which declares, "Weeping may last for the night, but a shout of joy comes in the morning" (Ps. 30:5 NASB). Shouts of joy! Yes, there've been many nights of weeping—then and since—but the shouts of joy that have broken through the pain of grief have been incredible.

As you travel on, I pray that the words strung together across these pages have been words that bring you hope and joy for the journey. I wish I knew the end of your story and that I could tell you exactly how it's all going to pan out, but I simply can't. I can share the joys of my heart, the burdens that I've had to bear, and the stories of the women you've met amid these pages, and I can trust that God will bring you peace as you stay the course. While I don't know the outcome, I do know the Author, and I pray that as we come to a close in our time together amid these pages that you do, too. So, I ask again: do you know the Prince of Peace (appendix A)? May you find joy in Jesus, rest in His very great and precious promises, and entrust Him with every care of your mommy heart today.

My Pregnancy Prayer for You

God, You give us great reason to rejoice by the sacrifice of Your Son Jesus. In the darkest of times and the hardest of circumstances, we always have a reason to rejoice because of the salvation that You bring. I pray that You would overwhelm this woman with joy today. May You help her to see that true joy comes from You alone and cannot be tied solely to her circumstances. Give her eyes to see and a heart that recognizes the joy of this season of her life, as she prepares to welcome a new baby into the world, even when it may be scary. May she live Your will for her life, as Your Word says, praying continually, rejoicing always, and giving thanks in all things! Amen.

Joy No Matter What

pregnancy promise ————————————————

Jesus is our source of true joy.

Though the fig tree does not bud
    and there are no grapes on the vines,
though the olive crop fails
    and the fields produce no food,
though there are no sheep in the pen
    and no cattle in the stalls,
yet I will rejoice in the LORD,
    I will be joyful in God my Savior.
The Sovereign LORD is my strength;
    he makes my feet like the feet of a deer,
    he enables me to tread on the heights.

HABAKKUK 3:17–19

While having a routine prenatal visit during my last pregnancy, I vividly recall making a deliberate and intentional choice to love and praise God—no matter what. I was on my fifth pregnancy. I had two living children at home and two in heaven. At nearly fourteen weeks along, things had been progressing smoothly. My nurse practitioner wasn't able to find the heartbeat with the Doppler wand, and she left me in the room to myself for a minute or two while she went to get a sonographer who could do a quick ultrasound. I wasn't too worried, because I knew how accustomed they were to doing ultrasounds at this high-risk clinic.

As I sat in the exam room alone, I realized that something could, in fact, be wrong . . . again. I prayed to God while I waited to be taken back for an ultrasound. "Whatever happens, Lord, I will still love You." I repeated this declaration over and over until my nurse practitioner came back to get me for the ultrasound.

My baby's precious body showed up on the screen, and right away we knew she was gone. The sonographer, who had become a friend by now, gently said, "I'm so sorry . . ." That's when my heart sank. Tears poured out. We all cried. But once I could muster up the strength to speak, I recalled my prayer, and I said it aloud to these precious women who were with me in that room: "I still love You, God. I still love You! I still trust You. I'll still serve You. You are still my God!"

The pain of losing Riyah Mae was heart wrenching. Still, there is joy in following hard after God, even in the difficult times. In this case, God graced me with the strength to choose ahead of time to trust, to love, to serve, and ultimately to find my joy in Him. I could remain joyful in spite of my circumstance because of who God is, what He has done, and what I trusted Him to continue to do in and through me. You can choose to trust and rejoice in Him, too. He is ever faithful!

Dear Lord, I thank You for loving me so. Please give me faith to believe in You and claim joy, no matter what. Especially as I think about the remaining days of this pregnancy, Lord, I ask that You would help me to choose joy and enjoy this time. I want my joy to always be rooted in You, Jesus! It's in Your great name I pray. Amen.

pen the promise

Can you think of a time when you were able to be joyful in Jesus, despite a difficult circumstance? Write about that experience in your journal, followed by a prayer asking God to help you claim joy in a specific area of need.

Expecting with Hope

Rejoice Always!

pregnancy promise ————————————————

The Lord's nearness gives us great reason to rejoice.

Rejoice in the LORD always. I will say it again: Rejoice! Let your gentleness be evident to all. The Lord is near.

PHILIPPIANS 4:4–5

I love how the apostle Paul in his letter commands the Philippians to rejoice. Not only does he tell them to rejoice, but he declares, "I will say it again: Rejoice!" (Phil. 4:4). He tells them repeatedly to rejoice. Interestingly, he writes this letter while he himself is imprisoned; not typically a time when one would rejoice. Yet that's just the example he sets—that we can rejoice in the Lord, regardless of our circumstances. Reason being, the Lord is near.

Just as the Lord was with Paul all those years ago in the confines of a jail cell, He is with you and longs to free you from the chains that keep you in bondage, unable to experience a joy-filled relationship with Him. He was with you before, He is with you now, and He will be with you tomorrow. If you know Jesus as your Savior, one day you will meet Him face-to-face. This is great reason to rejoice! As you walk this journey of pregnancy after loss, remember who God is and that He is near, regardless of what's happened in the past or how you feel today. "His love endures forever" (Ps. 136:1).

Heavenly Father, in You there is great reason to rejoice. Help me, Lord, to be like the apostle Paul, who continually praised and worshipped You, in spite of the many trials he faced: imprisonment, persecution, and threats on his very life. My worries and fears seem trivial in light of what he endured, but I know, Lord, that You care about every aspect of my life and every burden of my heart. Please fill my heart with joy that overflows and is evident in and through my life. Amen.

pen the promise ——————————————

Paul tells us to "rejoice in the Lord always." Write a reaction to this command in your journal. Be honest. If it seems impossible to genuinely rejoice, tell God so in prayer and ask Him to draw you near.

Expecting with Hope

Choose Joy Today

pregnancy promise ————————————————

There's something to rejoice about each day.

The LORD has done it this very day; let us rejoice today and be glad.

PSALM 118:24

When I became pregnant with Aiyana, a year after Chloe had died, I remember how much emphasis I tended to place on those milestone moments: the twenty-week ultrasound, the movement within, and ultimately the birth. I let emotions rule much of the time and based my joy on my circumstances. It was an easy thing to do, but a miserable place to be.

From a biblical perspective, we ought to be joyful regardless of our circumstances, because of who Jesus is and what He has done for us. Our key verse reminds us that we have something to rejoice about daily—the fact that we are here, living, and that the Lord has made this day! In that alone, we ought to rejoice and be glad.

Too often, fears, worries, and discontent steal our joy. When you wallow in the pain of your past, it's impossible to embrace joyful anticipation of the baby who is truly already here, living inside of you as you carry this precious child, awaiting his/her physical birth. Is not the miracle that this baby is living, growing, and thriving reason enough to rejoice? That truth alone is cause for celebration. Relish in the moment, count your blessings, and give thanks to God.

Dear Lord, You give us many reasons to rejoice. I confess that I often overlook the blessings of my day and too easily become entangled in the worry of my circumstances. Lord, I pray that You would change my perspective. Bring to mind those things that I have great reason to rejoice over. Give me eyes to see with gladness the beauty of this moment, this day. Amen.

pen the promise ———————————————

Count your blessings, literally. Write down in your journal as many things as you can think of that you have to be thankful for today. Pray and give thanks to God for the blessing of this day.

Filled with Joy

pregnancy promise ───────────────────

The Lord can fill you with joy.

The LORD has done great things for us, and we are filled with joy.

PSALM 126:3

Nichelle struggled with years of infertility, the loss of her stillborn son Elijah, and a miscarriage. She got to a point in life where it was difficult to find joy in anything. So many of the pleasures in life prior to these experiences now only brought about grief and pain. She questioned, "How could I enjoy anything ever again when a piece of me was missing?"

She recalled this time in her life and shared a story of how a simple glass jar became a turning point for her:

> One day while cleaning my house I went to dust an old blue Ball glass Mason jar. For a moment I thought, what if I put something in here that I was grateful for? I thought, even if small, I could see that something brought me joy or gratefulness. So, I created the Joy Jar. . . . Slowly, I began to see joy in my life again.

Over time, I imagine Nichelle's jar filled with tokens and recorded notes that reminded her of joy.

Let's consider ourselves to be that glass jar, and despite our circumstances, take a look at the many blessings that surround us and count them as joy. The Lord can fill the empty places with joy as we look to see His loving hand in our lives. Perhaps it's a blessing of provision, a measure of peace, or a blanket of comfort. How is the Lord filling your joy jar—your heart—with more of Him today?

Dear Lord, You have done great things! Help me not lose sight of all You have done for me, the foremost of which is enduring the shame of the cross so that I could be set free. Help me to be filled with joy in You, Jesus. Help me to see the wonders You have done right in my midst, beyond the pain of my past and transcending the worries of my present. Help me to count my blessings to overflowing. Amen.

pen the promise ————————————————

Create a Joy Jar of your own! Keep a pen and scrap paper next to it to write down things that bring you joy.

Joyful in Hope

pregnancy promise ————————————————

God desires for you to be joyful in hope.

Be joyful in hope, patient in affliction, faithful in prayer.

ROMANS 12:12

Whether she knew it or not, I was Jayme's biggest fan, cheering her on from the sidelines as she awaited the arrival of her second living child into this world. She had one little guy in her care at home, and a precious daughter who had gone to be with Jesus due to a terminal diagnosis in utero. I didn't have the opportunity to get to know Jayme personally, but I met her in person once and knew of her situation. We corresponded by email and kept up to speed through social media.

What I can say about Jayme is that she exudes the joy of Jesus like I haven't seen in too many others. Her joy is contagious, her perspective is inspiring, and her faith overflows with hope. When I think about examples of people who do as Romans 12:12 commands—to be joyful in hope, patient in affliction, and faithful in prayer—Jayme comes to mind.

This verse also causes me to pause and examine myself by asking, Am I joyful in hope, patient in affliction, and faithful in prayer? Why not do the same in light of your current pregnancy? If you aren't doing as this verse commands, it's time to consider what changes need to be made, what sin needs to be confessed, and what burdens need to be laid down at the foot of the cross in surrender.

It's hard to be joyful when the pain of our past creeps in. It's difficult to be patient when we'd much rather skip over the waiting and just forge ahead to our desired outcome. For these reasons, and more, it is so important that we be faithful in prayer. Pour out your heart to God in prayer, sweet friend, and let Him carry your burden so that, like Jayme, you can press on with joyful hope, patience, and a faithfulness that inspires others.

I'm sure you are wondering. Jayme gave birth to a healthy baby boy this past year. My, oh my, does he have a full head of hair, each one of which God has numbered (Matt. 10:30).

Father in Heaven, You are the God of all hope who brings great joy and peace. Instill in me a patient heart that is faithful in prayer. When worry sets in because of my painful experience of previous loss, help me to refocus my thoughts on the joy and hope You bring. Amen.

pen the promise ──────────────────

Are you currently joyful in hope, patient in affliction, and faithful in prayer? What is one step you can take today that would help you live out this command?

Appendix A

Meet the Prince of Peace

Do you know the Prince of Peace?

As the prophet Isaiah foretold of the coming Messiah, he wrote, "For to us a child is born, to us a son is given, and the government will be on his shoulders. And he will be called Wonderful Counselor, Mighty God, Everlasting Father, Prince of Peace" (Isa. 9:6).

Prince of Peace. King Jesus. Wonderful Counselor. Mighty God. This is Jesus, our Prince of Peace. Do you *know* Him? To know the Prince of Peace means:

> We acknowledge the fact that we are all sinners. "For all have sinned and fall short of the glory of God" (Rom. 3:23).
>
> We know there's a price that must be paid for sin. "For the wages of sin is death" (Rom. 6:23).
>
> We believe that Jesus Christ, the Prince of Peace, died to pay the penalty for our sins. "But God demonstrates his own love for us in this: While we were still sinners, Christ died for us" (Rom. 5:8).
>
> We understand that God wants to save us from our sins. "If you declare with your mouth, 'Jesus is Lord,' and believe in your

heart that God raised him from the dead, you will be saved" (Rom. 10:9).

We are sure of an eternity in heaven that awaits us. "Everyone who calls on the name of the Lord will be saved" (Rom. 10:13).

Making Peace with God in Prayer . . .

Dear heavenly Father, thank You for loving me unconditionally. Thank You for making a way to You through Your Son Jesus, the Prince of Peace. Lord, I know from Your Word that we all fall short of Your glory. This includes me, God. I humbly admit to You now that I am a sinner in need of a Savior.

Thank You, Jesus, for paying the penalty that I deserved by dying on the cross and bearing the weight of my sin. I believe in my heart that You are Lord and that God, the Father, raised You from the dead so that I might have an abundant life in You. I ask You now, Jesus, to enter into my heart and take over. Be the Lord of my life so that I may now have peace with God. I trust You with all that I am, and I love You because You have first loved me. May Your peace rule in my heart always, as I rejoice in the salvation that You bring. Amen.

If you have genuinely entered into a saving relationship with Jesus Christ, the Prince of Peace, I would love to rejoice with you! Please tell me about it by emailing me at: teske@mommieswithhope.com.

Expecting with Hope

Appendix B

Coping with Prenatal Diagnosis & Adverse Health Issues

Pregnancy and childbirth are nothing short of a miracle. Countless things have to go right in order for a baby to grow and develop in the womb and be born living and healthy. As you and I well know, pregnancy in and of itself does not guarantee the birth of a healthy baby. Sometimes, pregnancy ends in miscarriage, stillbirth, or loss after birth. Other times, prenatal diagnosis of medical anomalies or health concerns are brought to light during pregnancy. Parents also may have to deal with premature birth, NICU stays, and various health matters that manifest after birth. While medical technology and advancements are a wonderful blessing in so many ways, the knowledge that we gain from such technology can also bring to light a number of issues and complexities that, a generation ago, we wouldn't have even known about.

If you are facing the news of prenatal diagnosis, enduring bed rest due to medical issues for yourself or your baby, or realizing that you will be caring for a child with special needs, please know resources and support are available to you. Visit the Mommies with Hope website and check out "Resources" for more information. www.mommieswithhope.com

Appendix C

When Loss Happens Again

I'm guessing you opened the pages to this book with some degree of trepidation due to a painful pregnancy history. It is my prayer that you are reading this appendix—*When Loss Happens Again*—merely out of curiosity, and not based on personal need. But I would be naïve to think that another loss is beyond the realm of possibility. In fact, I am keenly aware of this very real and difficult experience, having three babies in heaven myself. As a mom who's been there and who doesn't want anyone else to ever have to go there, my heart goes out to you. I pray that you find the following resources to be of help and of hope to you on your healing journey.

Recommended Resources and Support

If you're walking through the tragedy of loss, yet again, I recommend the following books:

Avella, Becky. *And Then You Were Gone: Restoring a Broken Heart after Pregnancy Loss*. Enumclaw, WA: Pleasant Word, 2010.

Drake, Teske. *Hope for Today, Promises for Tomorrow: Finding Light Beyond the Shadow of Miscarriage or Infant Loss*. Grand Rapids, MI: Kregel Publications, 2012.

MacArthur, John. *Safe in the Arms of God: Hope from Heaven About the Death of a Child.* Nashville, TN: Thomas Nelson, 2003.

I invite you to also visit the Mommies with Hope website for additional resources and support:

www.mommieswithhope.com

Appendix D

About Mommies with Hope

Mommies with Hope is a biblically based support group ministry for women who have experienced pregnancy or infant loss. Basing their ministry on 2 Corinthians 1:3–4, the founders of Mommies with Hope, Teske Drake and Lindsay Farmer, desired to comfort others with the same comfort that they received from God, and the group began meeting in the fall of 2007.

Mommies with Hope has grown to minister to men and women around the world through online support communities—Expecting with Hope (pregnancy after loss support); Waiting with Hope (infertility support); and Daddies with Hope (support for fathers)—in addition to the support group meetings that take place in the Midwest. You can find additional online support for each of the following needs at www.mommieswithhope.com.

Mommies with Hope—support for those grieving after miscarriage, stillbirth, or infant loss.

Expecting with Hope—support for those pregnant after loss.

Waiting with Hope—support for those struggling with infertility.

Daddies with Hope—support for fathers after miscarriage, still-birth, or infant loss.

Acknowledgments

With heartfelt gratitude, I thank the wonderful team at Kregel for embracing the vision for this book and recognizing the unique needs of the women for whom I write. Dennis, Steve, Dawn, Sarah, Beth, Leah, Adam, and Noelle—thanks for ministering alongside me.

To my agent, Ann Byle of Credo Communications, you are a true blessing! I can't imagine anyone else being alongside me on this writing journey. Thank you isn't enough.

To the ladies and fellow leaders of Mommies with Hope ministry, it's a joy to serve you and to serve alongside you. You've ministered to me in more ways than you know over the years. Much love to you all!

To my cherished godly girlfriends who have prayed me through the writing of this book (and then some)—Amy, Beth, Brittney, Deb, Jen D., Jen S., Kelsey, Keri, Lindsay, Mindy, Susan, and Tara—I am so grateful for each one of you. Your prayers were felt, your encouragement is priceless, and your friendship is a true blessing. Pastor Dave, while you may not be one of the girls, you are a wonderful encourager, prayer warrior, and supporter of the ministry and of me. Thank you! To my Growth Group at Lakeside Fellowship—every word of encouragement, every prayer, and every challenge has blessed me to pieces.

To those of you who so graciously shared your stories, your hearts, your struggles, and your victories—Betsy, Holly, Jessica, Kim, Kristi, LeeAnn, Meri, Mindy, Nichelle, Patricia, Sandy, Sarah, Sheralyn,

Sonya—I am indebted to you. This book wouldn't have been possible without your voices. Thank you, thank you, thank you!

Mom, thanks for always believing in me and for being my biggest fan. Your loving support means the world to me and it's pretty amazing to have a mom for a best friend. I can only hope to be my daughter's best friend when she is grown. I love you!

To Justin—releasing three babies to heaven and welcoming two on earth will always be a cherished chapter of our life's story. I love you for the father you are.

To Gabe and Aiyana—my two miracle children—I love you both the most. Through you two, I am blessed beyond measure. I never knew the Lord could give me so much love to share!

Jesus, You are my Prince of Peace. May the stringing together of my words always be saturated in the Word, which brings hope and gives life forevermore. All glory to You, Lord!

About the Author

Inspired by her own experience through the loss of her newborn daughter, Chloe, in 2006, Teske Drake cofounded Mommies with Hope, a biblically based support group ministry for women who have experienced the loss of a child (miscarriage, stillbirth, or infant loss), established in 2007, and currently serves as president. In 2009, Teske experienced the miscarriage of Jesse at six weeks gestation, and Riyah Mae at fourteen weeks gestation. Drawing from her personal experiences with miscarriage and infant loss, in addition to the similar experiences of the many women to whom she has ministered, Teske has a passion for sharing the hope of Jesus Christ in coping with loss.

Teske Drake has earned her PhD in Human Development and Family Studies from Iowa State University, where she focused her research primarily on women's experiences with miscarriage and infant loss, and most recently their support experiences after loss through the Mommies with Hope ministry. Her professional experience consists of teaching courses in child and family development at the university level as well as serving as former director of Hamilton's Academy of Grief and Loss, where she worked to provide grief-related information, education, resources, and support to grieving children, families, and the community in central Iowa and across the state. Teske is the author of *Hope for Today, Promises for Tomorrow: Finding Light Beyond the*

Shadow of Miscarriage or Infant Loss. She has written numerous articles and resources related to pregnancy and infant loss.

Teske and her family reside in central Iowa, serving the Lord with joy through their church, Lakeside Fellowship.

About the Author